Try single person in rocker. Seesaw with bigger figures and shorter length.

Piano Player.

River Boat

WHIRLIGIGS IN SILHOUETTE

Anders S. Lunde

Jan 2004

Try

Rooster Pecking P. 82

Blacksmith P-87

KC Publishing, Inc.
Kansas City, MO

Copyright © 1989 by Anders S. Lunde
All Rights Reserved.
Published by KC Publishing, Inc.,
Kansas City, Missouri   (816) 531-5730
Editing and production by Ramsey & Associates
Front cover photograph by Scott Cook
Back cover and body photographs by Richard Beckman
Technical illustrations by James Sexton

Instructions have been carefully checked for accuracy and the projects for safety. The publisher, however, cannot be responsible for human error, misinterpretation of directions or the differences in individual craftsmen's expertise.

First Edition

Printed in the United States of America

Library of Congress Cataloging-in-Publication Data
Lunde, Anders S.
    Whirligigs in Silhouette / Anders S. Lunde.
        p. cm.
    Includes index.
    ISBN 0-86675-013-4:$19.95 — ISBN 0-86675-014-2 (pbk.): $14.95
    1. Wooden toy making.   2. Whirligigs. I. Title.
T174.5.W6L87 1989
745.592-dc20   89-12675
                                          CIP

Dedication:

"To my wife"

CONTENTS

FORWARD

Through the years people have asked me how to make old-fashioned mechanical whirligigs like the Mule Kicking the Farmer, Man Cranking Car, and the like. When I began building them, I soon saw that they shared the same basic designs for the platform, the drive shaft, and the propeller. This simplified construction for all the models. I call them silhouette whirligigs because they are usually flat and can best be seen from the side. In addition to mechanical whirligigs I have included several non-mechanical weathervane whirligigs because they are similar to the silhouette type. A few of the designs are traditional, others I created. I have made all of the whirligigs in this book and they work.

I thank whirligig-makers across the country who have shared my enthusiasm for these fascinating objects of folk art. I also wish to thank the many readers of my books who have helped revive an interest in traditional American whirligigs.

—Andy Lunde

1

SILHOUETTE WHIRLIGIGS

Whirligigs

Whirligigs have been around for hundreds of years. Middle Age tapestries show children playing with hobby horse whirligigs with 4-bladed propellers at the end. George Washington, riding back to Mt. Vernon at the conclusion of the Revolution, brought some "whilagigs" for Martha's grandchildren in his saddle bags. In the late 18th and early 19th centuries, human figures waving their arms, swords, shovels, and other implements, were popular whirligigs. Then there were Indians in canoes, mallards and other birds, and windmills.

Sometime during the last hundred years whirligigs became more complicated. Mechanical whirligigs, harnessing the power of the wind, made things move and copied human activities such as chopping and sawing wood, churning butter, feeding animals, riding horses, and performing circus acts.

Essentially the whirligig is a wind toy or wind machine. It twists and turns in the wind, and there is a propeller connected with it somewhere, either as a power source or as a decoration.

Historically, there are four identifiable types of whirligigs. Arm-wavers twirl their arms while twisting in the wind. Winged whirligigs, birds real or imaginary, spin their wings in opposite directions while remaining sideways to the wind. Weathervane types always point into the wind; a propeller or other moving part makes them whirligigs.

Mechanical whirligigs use propellers to power an activity through drive shafts, gears, and connecting rods. Any wind propeller attached to something made to turn in the wind may be called a whirligig, and any accumulation of wind propellers on a frame that moves in the wind is certainly a whirligig. So many whirligigs defy classification. This book deals with simple silhouette whirligigs, mostly mechanical, but also with a few weathervanes.

Silhouette Whirligigs

Silhouette whirligigs have a distinct identity. They are two-dimensional, or relatively flat, wind toys or windmills. Most are mechanical because they are powered by a wind propeller turning a drive shaft which moves things about. Some are non-mechanical and turn to face the wind which enables their propellers to turn. These propellers may take the form of wheels, windmill sails, or decorative propellers. Silhouette whirligigs are sometimes referred to as cut-outs because their simple patterns can easily be cut out of thin wood. Nevertheless they can be as complicated as their designer wants them to be, and some take many hours to construct.

Silhouette whirligigs are very popular and are the easiest of the mechanical types to make. They have been around for at least a century and some of the designs were familiar to our great grandfathers. Some of the best known whirligigs have been the Man Chopping

Wood, Man Sawing Wood, Mule Kicking the Farmer, Milking the Cow, and Girl at the Pump.

There are many patterns and variations for silhouette whirligigs. For example, there are many ways to make the popular Mule Kicking the Farmer. In one design the legs are loose and swing as the mule body swings, in another the farmer's torso is balanced with a counter-weight so that the mule's kick sends him swinging. In still another, two connecting rods move both the farmer and the mule. Then there are alternative features: the farmer stands in front of either a barn or a hay pile, he is shoveling or pitching hay, or the figure may be the farmer's wife. The whirligig maker creates his or her own interpretation of events.

Construction is relatively easy because the silhouette whirligig is principally a cut-out design. Such a whirligig is best appreciated when seen silhouetted against the sky where its unceasing activity takes on a life of its own.

Whirligigs in This Book

The basic silhouette whirligig designs in this collection are easy to make. Some are familiar designs; others I have created. Specific measurements for each model, and drawings provide details. You can make the model as described, or you can alter the model or features to suit yourself. Better still, you can draw your own model and make a unique whirligig.

The whirligigs in this book have been classified according to their principal characteristics, as follows:

Moving Torso Whirligigs

These whirligigs show men and women in action. The upper body is balanced between two legs so that the connecting rod moves the body forward and backward seeming to produce additional activity. In the Man/Woman-Fishing, the upper body action includes moving the fishing rod back and forth although no independent action of the arms is required. In Baking a Pie the more complex torso action moves separate arms along the table with a rolling pin. Many early American mechanical whirligigs were of this type, including the familiar Man Sawing Wood and Man Chopping Wood.

Rocking Whirligigs

Although related to Moving Torso types, the Rocking whirligigs developed a rocking motion primarily. They were usually well balanced, requiring little power. For example, in the Equestrienne the horse and rider are suspended in the middle and simply rock up and down. The problem was finding the most efficient position for the connecting rod. The Oil Well Pump, on the other hand, is so balanced that it will move in a light wind with a relatively small propeller.

Hidden Drive Shaft Whirligigs

These whirligigs are distinguished by having drive shafts that operate within the platform which acts as their support. To make them otherwise would involve more space and additional supporting brackets. Several cams may be used and more than one action can take place with this mechanism. While the action may be similar to the preceding types, the operation is usually more complex. In Chickens Feeding the drive shaft is long and two cams are placed in such a way that the action is complementary: one chicken goes up while the other goes down.

Single Arm Whirligigs

These whirligigs are so designed to make one part of the body or object move repetitively. While the action is simple, the situation makes it significant, as in the case of the soldier saluting the flag.

Double Arm Whirligigs

Like the single arm whirligigs these models make essentially one movement but two arms are involved. In more complicated whirligigs, the arms may be made to produce separate and additional actions. For example, in one whirligig I designed one arm waves an object in the air while the other arm pulls a chain which activates another figure.

Double Cam Whirligigs

In these whirligigs, double-cam does not refer to two cams, but to two which are constructed next to each other. One goes up as the other goes down. This action enables the farmer's hands to move authentically in Milking the Cow. In this whirligig, as in several others, a platform extension is made to accommodate the figure involved in the action.

Weathervane Whirligigs

Weathervane whirligigs have a propeller turning on them, and are designed to face the wind. In Dutch Tulips, the windmill turns; in the Valentine a propeller with heart-shaped blades turns. Any vane, even a propeller on a stick, can be made into a weathervane whirligig.

As you work with these models you will begin to imagine other actions of humans, animals, or objects which can be made into whirligigs by adapting the mechanisms and movements in new ways. At that point you will begin to develop an insight into the creative experience of whirligig making.

2

SILHOUETTE WHIRLIGIG COMPONENTS

Components

The three basic parts of silhouette whirligigs are the platform, the driving mechanism, and the propellers. They are essentially the same for all whirligigs. There are some variations in final shape of the platform according to individual taste. The final propeller design will depend on the power requirements of the individual whirligig and local wind conditions. When the platform is completed and the location of the components of the whirligig are marked on it, the other parts are easily fitted on. Details on additional materials (axles, connecting rods, wires, nuts, brads, screws, etc.) are listed with each model.

This chapter details the basic construction of all the whirligigs in this book. In the following chapters where different models are described, only variations from principal measurements or changes in design are mentioned.

Platform

The wooden platform (Fig. 2-1) is the main frame of the whirligig. The standard platform measures approximately 3/4 x 2-1/4 x 24 in. for most models. Changes in platform size occur in some models.

The design can be made more attractive by cutting off a section of the rear of the platform, or shaping it. If no structure or mechanism is involved, trim the end of the platform to 1 in. (from 2-1/4), taking care to not interfere with the pivot sock-

et. Further improvements in platform design are made by adding a platform extension, described later. Lay out all the details before cutting for design improvement.

Mark off the points on the platform where each item or figure will be placed. In model directions, all measurements are given from the front of the whirligig platform. Drill the 3/8 in. pivot socket not more than 2 in. deep; it is usually located 4 to 7 in. from the front end of the platform. In the drawings the pivot socket is represented by the letter "P", meaning "Pivot."

Where figures or objects are secured by screws from the bottom of the platform, first drill a 3/8 in. diameter hole 1-1/2 in. deep, and complete the hole with a 3/16 in. bit to allow for the passage of a No. 6 flathead screw 1-1/4 or 1-1/2 in. long. If a plywood tail is required, cut a 1/4 in. tail slot to the required length, at the rear of the platform. If a metal tail is called for, cut a coping saw slot.

When support pieces must be attached to the sides of the platform, draw guidelines 3/4 or 1 in. below the top edge of the platform. Attach the pieces with carpenter's glue and 1/2, 3/4, 1, or 1-1/4 in. brads. Drilling pilot holes for brads will prevent splitting the wood.

After the pivot socket is drilled, place a metal lining in the hole to reduce wear caused by the whirligig revolving on the spindle. Many whirligig makers use copper tubing for whirligigs of this size.

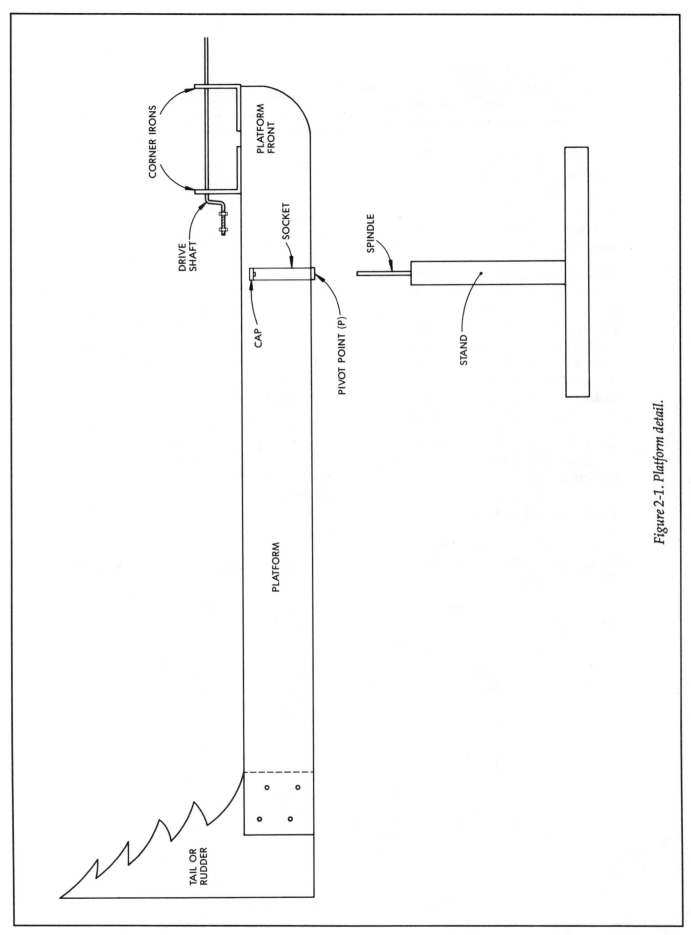

Figure 2-1. Platform detail.

13

Any tubing you have on hand that will do the job is acceptable. The 2 in. tension pin, 3/8 in. in diameter, available at any hardware store, is an inexpensive ready-made socket liner. In the text and illustrations the 3/8 in. pivot socket hole referred to is for the 2 in. tension pin. If you use other types of tubing, use the proper diameter bit for the socket hole and metal spindles that fit the pivot socket (Fig. 2-2).

A metal cap should be placed in the bottom of the socket for the spindle to ride on, or the spindle could drill itself through the platform. The cap can be made of the point of a rounded 20d nail hammered into the bottom of the hole. A small screw may also be used. If a tension pin is used as the liner, use the head of a 16d nail, fitted into the top of the pin.

The tail may now be attached with nails and glue. The platform is ready for the driving mechanism.

Driving Mechanism

The driving mechanism consists of the support brackets, drive shaft, and connecting rod or wire.

Support brackets

The support brackets are two standard 1-1/2 in. corner irons. When in place, the top hole of each corner iron is about 1 in. from the base. Drill small pilot holes, then place the first bracket at the front of the platform so that it protrudes slightly. The position of the rear bracket may vary depending on the model being constructed, but the standard will be 3-1/2 in. from the front of the platform. On corner irons the screw holes are either centered or off-centered. Be sure to get the irons with holes that are centered. The off-centered irons can be used but they must face the same way on the platform so the holes can line up. These may be slightly off-center but the drive shaft will work.

An alternative to having two corner irons hold the drive shaft is the grooved or slotted block, called the Platform Extension (Fig. 2-3). This makes a more pleasing design, especially when the shape of the extension is incorporated into the platform itself, as shown in the drawings of Man/Woman Fishing and Baking a Pie. To make the extension, cut

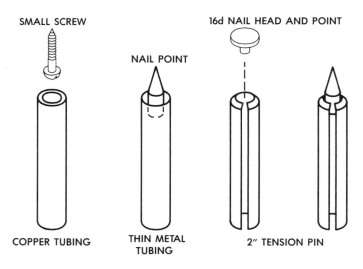

SMALL SCREW

NAIL POINT

16d NAIL HEAD AND POINT

COPPER TUBING

THIN METAL TUBING

2" TENSION PIN

Figure 2-2. Pivot socket liners and caps.

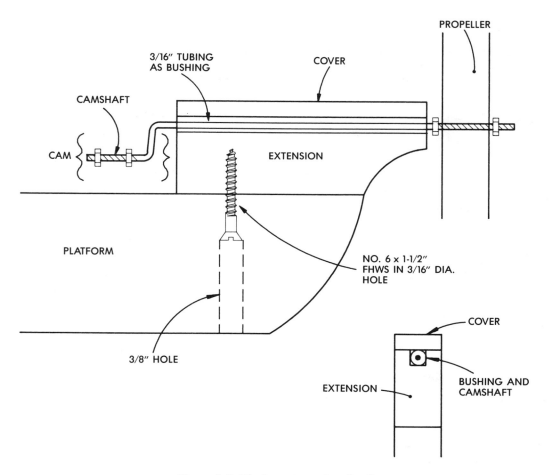

Figure 2-3. Platform extension detail.

out a piece of wood 3/4 x 1-1/4 x 4 in. Cut a 3/16 in. wide and 3/16 in. deep groove along the top for the drive shaft. Make a cover 1/4 x 3/4 x 4 in.

Attach the platform extension with glue and either nails driven in from above through the groove or with a 1-1/2 in. No. 6 screw turned from the bottom. Drill guide or pilot holes first. Place 3/16 in. brass tubing in the slot and glue/brad the cover over it. In longer extension pieces or slotted blocks for drive shafts, smaller one-inch pieces of tubing may be placed at each end of the slot, as in the See-Saw and Chickens Feeding whirligigs.

Sometimes the drive shaft is not yet needed, but add the drive shaft at this point if objects are being added to the platform that will interfere with the insertion of the drive shaft. Also add the necessary washers and nuts to the threaded drive shaft. Spacers to keep the propeller blades away from the platform are not necessary when platform extensions are used.

Drive shaft

The drive shaft (Fig. 2-4) is made of a 7-1/2 in. length of 1/8 in. metal rod. The length may vary with the model but the ends will be threaded with a 6/32 die. A die and holder can be purchased at any hardware store for just a few dollars.

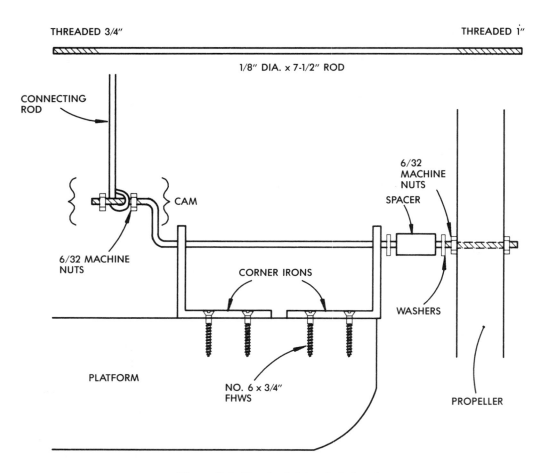

THREADED 3/4"

THREADED 1"

1/8" DIA. x 7-1/2" ROD

CONNECTING ROD

6/32 MACHINE NUTS

CAM

SPACER

6/32 MACHINE NUTS

6/32 MACHINE NUTS

CORNER IRONS

WASHERS

PLATFORM

NO. 6 x 3/4" FHWS

PROPELLER

Figure 2-4. Standard driveshaft detail.

The description "6/32" simply means that the wire size is 6 and that there are 32 turns per inch. Or 8 turns per 1/4 in., 16 per 1/2 in., and 24 per 3/4 in...but always double check. Thread the front end 1 in. (about 30 turns of the handle) and the rear end 3/4 in. (about 20 turns) (Fig. 2-5). Then make a 1/2 in. cam about 1 in. from the rear end. Use a vice to make a 1/2 in. bend in the metal rod, as shown (Fig. 2-6). Where more movement is required, a 3/4 or 1 in. cam is suggested. Do not damage the thread. Put two machine nuts on the front end for the propeller and two on the rear end for the connecting rod. Where a longer or different drive shaft is required directions for these will be included with the design.

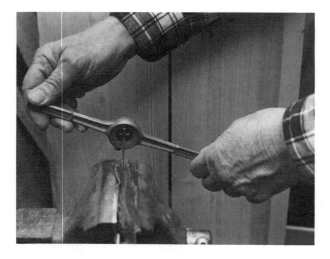

Figure 2-5. Thread drive shaft with a 6/32 die.

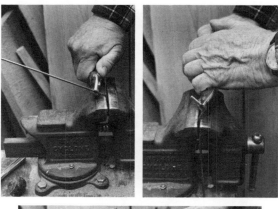

Figure 2-6. Use a vice to bend the cam.

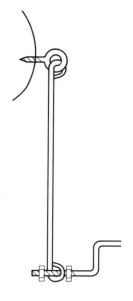

THE CONNECTING ROD MADE
OF 1/16" OR 3/32" BRASS
ROD, SECURED WITH 2 6/32
MACHINE NUTS AND ATTACHED
TO MOVING PARTS WITH 1/4"
OR 3/8" SCREW EYE.

Figure 2-7. Connecting rod and screw eye.

Connecting rod

The connecting rod is made of firm wire which is turned loosely around the drive shaft on one end and attached to a screw eye on a figure on the other. Check carefully because the connecting rod can jam up the mechanism if it is not properly attached. Two machine nuts glued in position on the drive shaft will hold the wire in place. A brass rod of 1/16 in. diameter makes a good connecting rod; the length will vary with each design. Use a 3/32 in. rod where greater strength is required. Connecting rods are attached to moving parts from the drive shaft by means of screw eyes. Screw eye sizes for these whirligigs are 1/4 and 3/8 in. (Fig.2-7).

Spacers and Collars

As you install the drive shaft, make sure that the cam at the rear end runs freely. The front end of the drive shaft will protrude about 2 in. beyond the front end of the platform when support brackets are used. There will usually be some space between the front corner iron/support bracket and the propeller. This space can be filled with a spacer or collar (Fig. 2-8). The spacer prevents the drive shaft from sliding back and disengaging the connecting rod. It also holds the propeller and cam in position.

To install a spacer, place the drive shaft so the cam is in position for the connecting rod to function properly. Measure the space between the front support bracket and the rear propeller nut, allowing for two washers. Cut a piece of 3/16 or 1/4 in. metal tubing to serve as a spacer. Place the spacer on the shaft before attaching the propeller.

Spacers can also be made from wooden beads, small spools, or blocks constructed by drilling 3/16 or 1/4 in. holes through small (about 1/2 x 1/2 x 5/8 in.) wood blocks. Where there is a closed cam, as in Chickens Feeding, drill the hole first, then saw the block in half

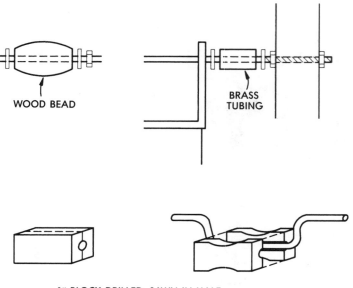

WOOD BEAD

BRASS TUBING

1" BLOCK DRILLED, SAWN IN HALF, AND GLUED AROUND CAM TO HOLD CONNECTING ROD

Figure 2-8. Types of spacers and collars.

lengthwise to fit. Glue the halves around the shaft. Cut notches in the middle of such collars for connecting rods.

Figure 2-9 shows the differences between the standard platform and the modified platform with the platform extension. The locations of the various components are also shown.

Propellers

I prepared a standard propeller, but found that because of the different tensions in the whirligig mechanisms and the varied wind velocities, it would be better to develop several propellers suited to different environments. They are:

Cross-lap propeller, 16 in. in
 diameter.
Maltese Cross propeller:
 -4 bladed, 11 in. and 13 in.
  diameter.

-2 bladed, 11 in. and 13 in.
 diameter.
Straight-bladed propeller, 4
 blades, 11 in. diameter.

Cross-Lap Propeller

Arms (2): 3/4" x 3/4" x 8"
Blades (4): 3" x 6" sheet metal
 (light or thin wood
 (1/8"-3/16")

To build the cross-lap propeller (Fig. 2-10), make a cross-lap joint of the arms as shown. In the center, drill a 7/64 in. hole for the 1/8 in. threaded drive shaft. Mark the ends of the arms for a 45-degree angle and, with a coping saw, cut down 2 inches. Trim and round off the ends with a file and insert the metal blades, securing them with small nails or brads. If wooden blades are used, simply cut off one-half of the slotted arms, exposing the same angled side, and glue/brad the blades in place.

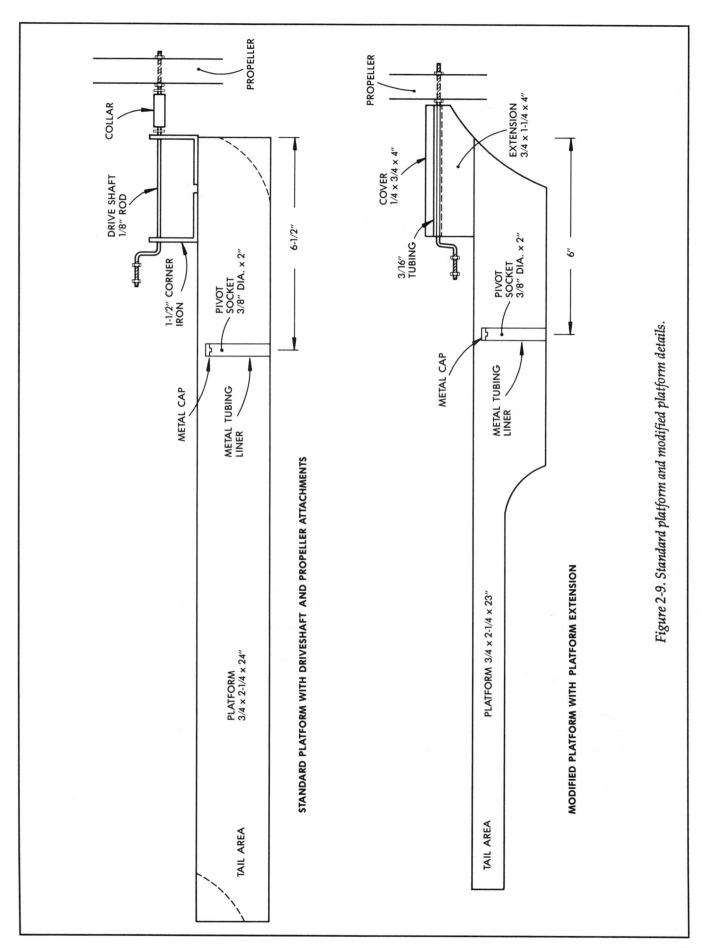

Figure 2-9. Standard platform and modified platform details.

19

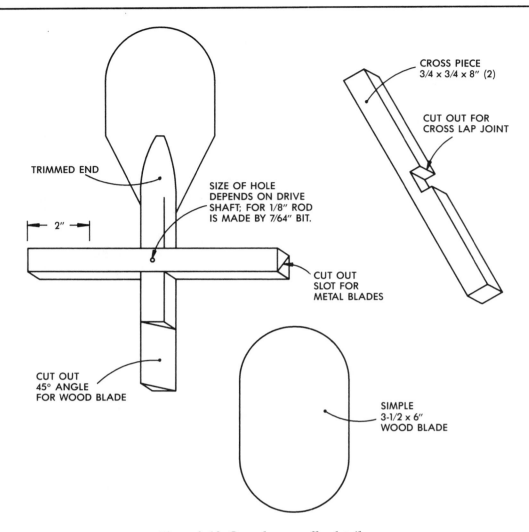

CROSS PIECE
3/4 x 3/4 x 8" (2)

CUT OUT FOR
CROSS LAP JOINT

TRIMMED END

SIZE OF HOLE
DEPENDS ON DRIVE
SHAFT; FOR 1/8" ROD
IS MADE BY 7/64" BIT.

2"

CUT OUT
SLOT FOR
METAL BLADES

CUT OUT
45° ANGLE
FOR WOOD BLADE

SIMPLE
3-1/2 x 6"
WOOD BLADE

Figure 2-10. Cross-lap propeller detail.

Maltese Cross Propeller

Hubs: 3/4" x 1-1/2" x 1-1/2"
    or 3/4" x 2" x 2"
Blades: 3/16" x 2" x 5"
    or 3/16" x 2" x 6"

The Maltese Cross propeller (Fig. 2-11) is a simple circular hub with blades. Mark off the hubs indicating the center point and draw center lines across both sides and edges. Draw 45-degree diagonal lines through the four edge centers. On the 1-1/2 in. hub, draw a 3/8 in. depth line for the blade slots; on the 2 in. hub, these lines are 1/2 in. deep. Drill a 7/64 in. hole in the center for the threaded 1/8 in. drive shaft. Use a miter saw and a coping saw to cut the blades to 1 in. at the hub and 2 in. at the ends. Measure for each blade; never trust to your eyes alone. Fit the blades snugly into the slots with glue (Fig. 2-12). The blades turn outward at the top, preventing them from striking the whirligig. The final product looks like a Maltese Cross.

Straight-Bladed Propeller

Hub: 3/4" x 1-1/2" x 1-1/2 in.
Blades: 3/16" x 1-1/8" x 5"

As in the Maltese Cross propellers, mark off the center points of the hub and draw 45-degree lines across the centers of the

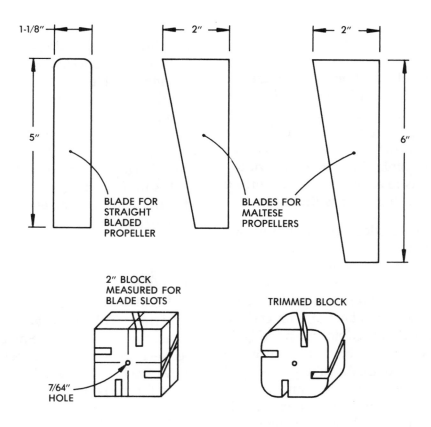

Figure 2-11. Maltese and straight-bladed propellers.

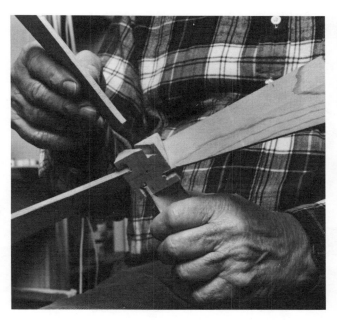

Figure 2-12. Fit the blades snugly into the slots.

sides for a straight-bladed propeller (Fig. 2-11). Cut out the slots 3/8 in. deep for the blades; insert the blades in the slots with glue. This propeller provides a steady power but is not as powerful as the other 4-bladed types.

You may need to construct a spacer to take up the slack between the front corner iron and the propeller. This is usually 1/2 to 3/4 in. long. Place washers on both ends of the spacer to guarantee free movement of the propeller. Put on a machine nut, and turn the propeller on the drive shaft. Secure the propeller with another machine nut in front. Spacers are usually not necessary for whirligigs with a platform extension in front.

Axles

Four types of axles (Fig. 2-13) are used as joints on the whirligigs in this book. They act as hip joints in some whirligigs permitting the upper part of the body to move back and forth between legs, as shoulder joints in others, providing movements to arms, and as supporting rods for rocking some whirligig parts.

The bent wire axle, with the ends turned down, is made of any wire or rod that can easily be bent with a pair of pliers. The bent wire axle most frequently used is the 3/32 in. brass rod with 1/8 in. tubing. The rod is bent at both ends to hold the body, arms, etc. in place (Fig. 2-14). It is not required that you use this size, or even to use the tubing liner. The liner saves wear and tear and ensures ease of movement. The bent wire axle is used on the Man/Woman Fishing and Fencing the Range whirligigs as hip joints.

The threaded rod axle is secured at the ends by nuts. Such axles are used at the hip and shoulder of the Girl at the Pump whirligig, and the hip, shoulder, and rolling pin of Baking a Pie. The usual threaded rod axle in this book is 1/8 in. in diameter and 2-1/8 in. long, and is threaded at both ends to a depth of 3/16 or 1/4 in. Threading is done with a 6/32 die and handle. The ends are secured with 6/32 nuts.

For double-arm mechanisms (Maestro at the Piano and Woman at the Computer), the 1/8 in. rod is threaded to 5/16 in. on each end to leave room for two nuts and an arm. This may take some fine measuring because there must be room between the nuts for the mechanism to move freely. The threading must leave room for the body.

In some instances, a regular machine screw threaded along its entire shank may be used as an axle. For example, in Girl at the Pump, the axles at the hands and the pump are 4/44 machine screws, 1-1/4 and 1-1/2 in. long, secured with nuts.

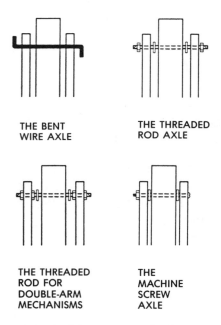

THE BENT
WIRE AXLE

THE THREADED
ROD AXLE

THE THREADED
ROD FOR
DOUBLE-ARM
MECHANISMS

THE
MACHINE
SCREW
AXLE

Figure 2-13. Four types of axles.

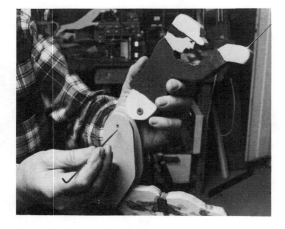

Figure 2-14. Installing a whirligig axle.

3

CONSTRUCTING SILHOUETTE WHIRLIGIGS

Tools and Materials

As the silhouette whirligig is principally a cut-out design, the woodwork involved is relatively easy and the metal work is not difficult. Only basic woodworking tools and a few metal working tools are required. Mechanical or electrical tools will simplify some jobs but are not entirely necessary. Early whirligig-makers worked with limited tools and rough wood.

Saws

A cross-cut hand saw and a coping saw are basic. A table saw, a band saw, a jig saw or a scroll saw will do the job more quickly.

Drill and Bits

A hand drill with selected bits usually found in a standard collection: 1/16, 7/64, 1/8, 3/16, and 1/4 in. Required sizes are mentioned in the instructions.

Other Wood Tools

Wood file, screw driver, pair of needle-nosed pliers, square, ruler, hammer, a vice suitable for wood working, and a small C-clamp.

Metal-Working Tools

You many need tin snips, 6/32 die with die holder, tubing cutter, a hack saw and a metal file.

The materials required are also basic and simple and may often be found around the house or in the workshop.

Wood

The platform and the figures are usually made of 3/4 in. lumber. Pine works well for whirligigs. Support pieces, such as legs which extend over the sides of the platform, are made of 1/4 in. plywood, as are most tails or rudders. Wooden propeller blades are sawed down to 1/8 or 3/16 in. thickness.

Steel or Brass Rods

Drive shafts and some axles will require 1/8 in. metal rods. Regular steel rods are available in hardware stores or metal supply shops. Welding rods and large drapery hangers found in dry-cleaning stores are useable. Brass rods can be purchased in hobby stores in 1 and 3 ft. lengths; these are preferable because they do not rust. Both steel and brass rods are easily cut with a hack saw. Stainless steel rods are less suitable because they are comparatively difficult to thread.

Threading the ends of the rods is suggested for the drive shaft and some axles. This is done with a 6/32 die in a die holder. File off any roughness on the end of the rod, round it off a little, and firmly turn the die on the rod until it holds. Then turn the handle the required number of times. On the die the number 32 means that 32 full turns will make an inch of thread. For the ends of drive shafts, I usually count 30 turns as one inch and 20 turns as 3/4 of an inch.

Rods in smaller sizes are used for some axles (like a 3/32 in. rod) and for connecting rods (1/16 in.). They may be of any metal, with brass preferred because it does not rust. These rods should be rigid but bendable with pliers.

Tubing

Three sizes of tubing are most frequently referred to in this book: 3/16 in., used to line drive shaft sockets in platform extension slots; 1/8 in., used to line holes for 3/32 in. rods used as bent axles; and 5/32 in. used with 1/8 in. threaded rods. The recommended tubing is made of brass and comes in 1 and 3 ft. pieces. Tubing may be cut with special metal saw blades, but never with a hack saw which leaves rough edges and may even bend thin tubing. It is best to use a tubing-cutter, obtainable in hardware stores and hobby shops.

Miscellaneous items

These include sandpaper, carpenter's glue, 1/2 and 3/4 in. brads or small nails, No. 6 1-1/4 and 1-1/2 inch flathead screws, 20d or 30d nails for spindles, 3/8 by 2 in. tension pins or other metal tubing for pivot socket lining, and screw eyes for connecting rods.

Materials to be used in each whirligig are described in the instructions.

General Procedures

Some standard steps will make whirligig construction easy and efficient. First, determine which whirligig to make and what tools and materials you need to make it. The steps listed below can generally be followed in making all whirligigs in this book.

1. Measure the base or platform and cut it out. Use a ruler, pencil, and square if necessary, to mark the locations of the holes, slots, and objects or figures that will be fixed to the platform (Fig. 3-1). Then drill the necessary holes and cut out the slots. Insert the socket liner (tension pin or tubing) in the pivot socket, and top it with a cap. Cut out the tail and glue/brad it in place if necessary. Attach the drive shaft support brackets. If required, cut and prepare a platform extension, then screw or nail it with glue to the front of the platform. The platform is now complete. It is also time to make at least a working stand for the whirligig.

2. Make the drive shaft as required by your model and as shown earlier. Thread the ends as necessary and make the cam(s) as required in the instructions. Place the drive shaft between the support brackets (or in the platform extension channel) to make sure that it is correct as to length and action (Fig. 3-2).

Figure 3-1. Mark the platform for the location of objects.

Figure 3-2. Installing the drive shaft on the platform.

Figure 3-3. Installing the propeller.

3. The propeller can be made now or last, but it should be considered at this stage. With the propeller attached it is easy to turn the drive shaft to see how things work (Fig. 3-3). Make the propeller suitable for your whirligig, as indicated with each model, taking local wind conditions into consideration.

4. Cut out the principal figures or objects, with their attached parts (arms, legs, supporting side pieces, etc.) (Fig. 3-4). Drill holes through the figures or objects where indicated and line the holes with brass tubing where recommended.

5. Assemble and attach the figures, beginning with the parts directly attached to the platform. In the instructions, measurements are given from the

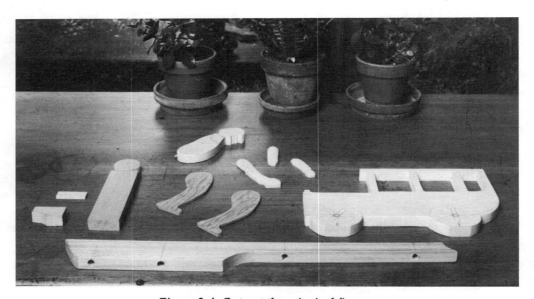

Figure 3-4. Cut out the principal figures.

front end of the platform proper, not including the extension. Start with the figure nearest the end of the drive shaft. Attach any permanent supporting pieces (side supports, skirts, legs). Attach the moving part to the standing or support pieces with an axle. Rock it back and forth to make sure it moves freely. If there is a slight binding, file down the side supports or figure. Or you can cut a small piece of wood or a 1/2 in. dowel to about 13/16 in. long and place it between the legs or support pieces just below the body (Fig. 3-5). This will widen the top opening and permit free movement of the body. Secure it with 1/2 in. brads.

6. Temporarily attach a connecting rod between the drive shaft and the screw eye on the figure. Turn the drive shaft to see if the movement is right. I use a stiff thin wire for this purpose and later make a more rigid connecting rod out of a heavier wire or brass rod.

7. Attach additional parts of the principal moving figure (arm with hammer, broom, fishing rod, etc.) with axles as needed, making sure they move properly. When the principal figure is complete, attach the next permanent feature (the anvil, fence post, farmer, etc.) after testing its location in relation to the moving figure. The hammer, for example, should stop about 1/2 in. above the anvil, the broom should not strike the husband, and so on.

8. Some whirligigs need extra adjustment at this point. The arms of the woman in the Baking a Pie whirligig have to work so that the rolling pin easily moves back and forth on the table as the upper part of her body moves to and fro. The Man/Woman Fishing whirligigs may lean too far forward and the extra weight may stop the entire mechanism. You can make a larger propeller to force the movement, but other solutions include shortening the connecting rod and thinning the arms down to reduce the weight. The arms of the Girl at the Pump must be connected to the pump handle so that the handle rises and falls with her body movement. In constructing any mechanical whirligig, adjustments usually have to be made, especially in the relationship of one moving part to another. These adjustments are part of the trial and error process of making whirligigs. Don't despair! Use your ingenuity to solve any problem. Your whirligig will work!

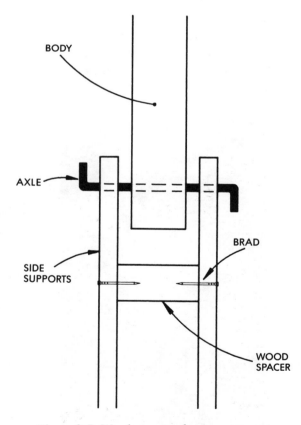

Figure 3-5. Wooden spacer between supports.

9. After secondary standing parts are in position, remaining standing figures or parts may be added. In the Fencing the Range whirligig, the workman holding the fence post cannot be added until the post is in place. In the Chickens Feeding whirligig, which has a different drive shaft arrangement, the final location and shape of the feed piles will depend on the pecking positions of the rooster and chick.

10. Finally, paint the whirligig (Fig. 3-6). Several different types of paint may be used, but I usually use oil paint for outdoor whirligigs, giving them two coats. You can add a coat or two of polyurethane varnish to assure weatherproofing. Sometimes an oil stain or watercolor may be applied to be finished off with polyurethane clear varnish. Otherwise, a glossy latex-acrylic paint is simplest to use because it dries quickly and cleans up easily with water. Whirligigs can be made to appear a cen-

tury-old by coating the painted whirligig with an antiquing toner or a dark varnish stain. Leave it on for a couple of minutes and then wipe it off. Some whirligig makers use loud colors which add to the humor of the piece. You will develop your own style of whirligig painting as you become more familiar with the techniques.

Making A Whirligig Stand

In general, mechanical whirligigs need stands with a wide base and a post high enough to keep the propeller clear (Fig. 3-7). A piece of 3/4 in. plywood about 8 x 8 in. can serve as the base for most whirligigs. A post 3/4 x 3/4 x 5 in. can be fitted into a 3/4 in. hole in the base with glue. Always check the height of the post with the propeller in place. A 20d or 30d nail can fit into a pilot hole drilled in the top of the post to serve as

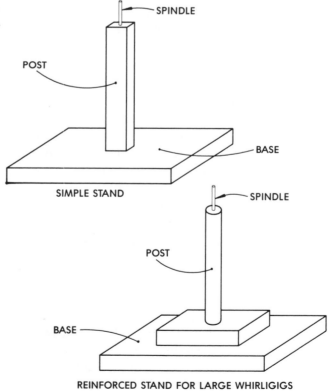

Figure 3-6. Painting your whirligig.

Figure 3-7. Two types of whirligig stands.

a spindle. For a wider base, you can glue and tack a larger piece of plywood to the bottom of a smaller base.

For most weathervane whirligigs, a smaller post may be used; those with overhanging propellers will require higher posts.

Displaying Your Whirligig

If you plan to exhibit your whirligig indoors, the stand as described above will do the job well. Or you may wish to make a more elaborate or finished one.

For outdoor display, first find a place in your yard where there is a good prevailing breeze. The whirligig can be mounted on a wooden post, preferably about 5 to 6 ft. high, using a 20d or 30d nail as a spindle (Fig. 3-8). A ready-made pole, about 1-1/4 in. thick, used for wooden drapery rods, can be purchased at the lumber yard. You can also use a 3/4 in. aluminum pole, 6 feet long,

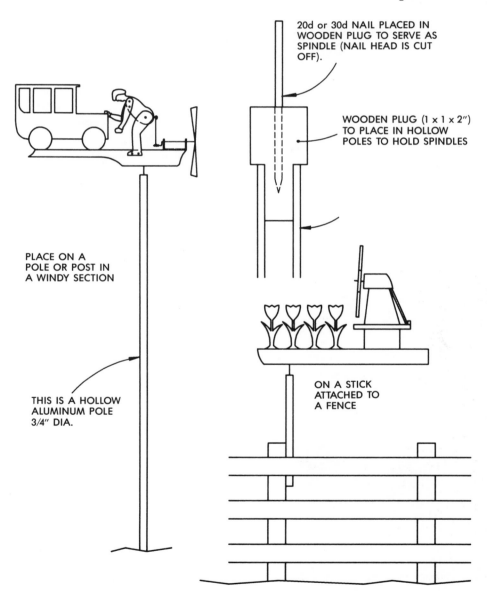

20d or 30d NAIL PLACED IN WOODEN PLUG TO SERVE AS SPINDLE (NAIL HEAD IS CUT OFF).

WOODEN PLUG (1 x 1 x 2") TO PLACE IN HOLLOW POLES TO HOLD SPINDLES

PLACE ON A POLE OR POST IN A WINDY SECTION

THIS IS A HOLLOW ALUMINUM POLE 3/4" DIA.

ON A STICK ATTACHED TO A FENCE

Figure 3-8. Ideas for displaying your whirligig.

which can easily be placed in the ground and looks attractive. A wood plug to hold the spindle must be prepared for such a pole as shown.

Other popular locations for whirligigs include fence posts or mail box posts, with a stick or pole added for height.

I must warn you that whirligigs exhibited at the roadside are in danger of being stolen. While this reflects on their value, it's not a pleasant event. I made my daughter a winged whirligig which she kept in the back yard of her farm. One day she decided to put it high on the signpost at the front entrance. The next day it was gone. That is why some whirligig owners take their more precious whirligigs indoors at night.

4

MECHANICAL SILHOUETTE WHIRLIGIGS

Figure 4-1. Cranking the Car whirligig.

Cranking the Car

The date of the Cranking the Car whirligig (Fig. 4-1), unlike most whirligigs, can readily be established. It belongs to the automobile era which began at the end of the 19th Century. The electric self-starter was first used in 1912 but did not become common until the 1930's. For some years thereafter the crank was used as a supplementary starter.

Most old cranking whirligigs have the driver on the side as a jointed figure with the drive shaft acting as a crank. Others have the drive shaft passing through or under the car while the cam acts as the crank. These whirligigs, however, do not show the action as it really occurred. I decided to create a whirligig which realistically shows the action in silhouette. The driver is going through the motions of cranking up the car with his stiff right arm; his left hand rests on the radiator. The auto is something I made up from my recollections of my father's 1935 Chevrolet.

MATERIALS

Platform: 3/4" x 2-1/4" x 22-1/4"
Extension: 3/4" x 1-1/4" x 2"
Cover: 1/4" x 3/4" x 2"
Gas Pump: 3/4" x 2" x 10"
Auto: 3/4" x 9" x 13"
Driver: Legs (2): 1/4" x 2-1/2" x 6"
   Torso: 3/4" x 2-1/2" x 7"
   Arms-right: 1/2" x 1-1/4" x 5"
    left-upper: 1/2" x 1" x 3-1/2"
     lower: 1/2" x 1" x 3-1/4"
Drive Shaft: 1/8" rod, 7-1/2" long,
   with 1/2" cam
Tension Pin: 2" long, 3/8" thick
   with cap
Tubing: 3/16", 4" long
Axle: 3/32" rod, about 3" long
Connecting Rod: 1/16" or 3/32"
   rod
Screw Eye: 3/8"

PROCEDURE

1. Cut out the platform and mark the locations of the objects that will be attached to it (Fig. 4-2). Drill a 3/8 in. hole for the tension pin and cap 6 in. from the front end of the platform. Drill holes for the screws which will hold the automobile in position at 13 and 20-1/2 in. from the front of the platform.

2. Cut out the platform extension, then cut a 3/16 x 3/16 in. slot for the drive shaft tubing, as instructed in the general procedures. Glue/brad the extension piece in position. Cut out the gas pump. Mark where the tubing will continue through the gas pump and drill a 3/16 in. hole through it. Screw the pump in place. Then glue/brad the cover in position.

3. Next, make and insert the standard drive shaft, as instructed in the general procedures.

4. Cut out the automobile. If you wish, carve out some of the details for highlighting. The model shows windows cut out. You may wish to place silhouettes of passengers in the car. Secure the auto in place with glue and 1-1/2 in. No. 6 flathead wood screws.

5. Cut out the parts of the driver. Drill a 3/32 in. hole through the center of the hip of one leg. The legs are mounted on the platform using glue and brads with the heels 6-1/4 in. from the front of the platform and the soles along a line 3/4 in. from the top edge of the platform. Holding the drill bit level and straight, drill through the first leg hole through the second leg. Drill a 1/8 in. hole through the torso hip and line it with tubing.

6. Mount the torso between the legs with a 3/32 in. brass rod. Position the right arm. Cut an angled piece out of the right shoulder so the hand will be in the center of the auto front. Test the arm as the torso moves to make sure it doesn't strike the car, then attach it to the torso with glue and brads. Drill small holes at the shoulder, elbow, and hand of the left arm pieces (Fig. 4-3). Hold the shoulder and hand in position with a 3/4 in. small roundhead screw and the elbows together loosely with wire. The joints should move freely.

7. If you have not already done so, make the drive shaft with a small cam (not more than 1/2 in.). Place a small screw eye in the tail of the torso and at-

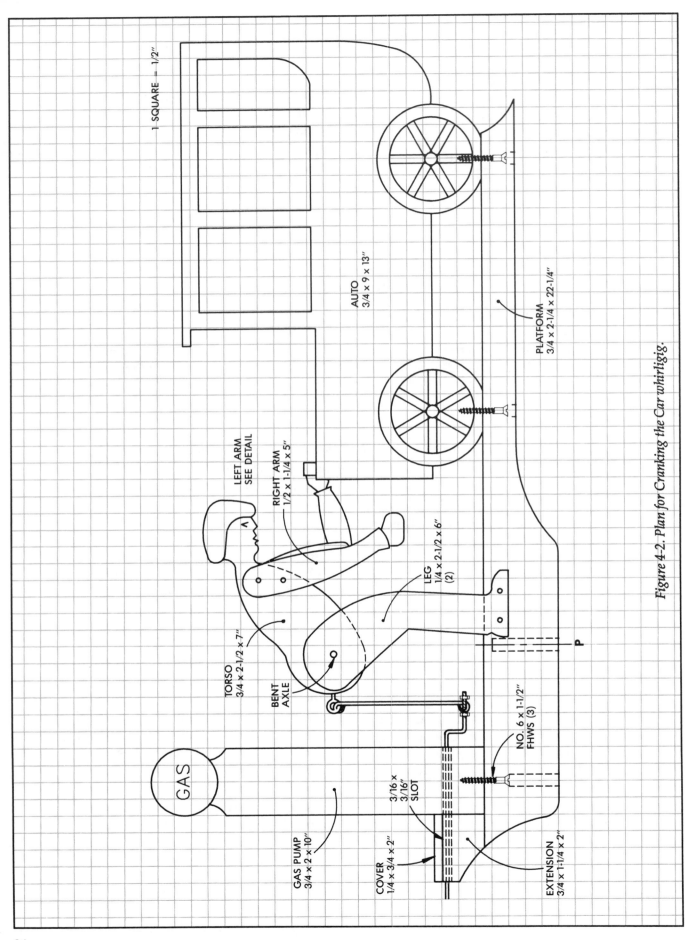

1 SQUARE = 1/2"

AUTO
3/4 x 9 x 13"

PLATFORM
3/4 x 2-1/4 x 22-1/4"

LEFT ARM
SEE DETAIL

RIGHT ARM
1/2 x 1-1/4 x 5"

LEG
1/4 x 2-1/2 x 6"
(2)

P

TORSO
3/4 x 2-1/2 x 7"

BENT
AXLE

GAS

NO. 6 x 1-1/2"
FHWS (3)

GAS PUMP
3/4 x 2 x 10"

3/16 x
3/16" SLOT

COVER
1/4 x 3/4 x 2"

EXTENSION
3/4 x 1-1/4 x 2"

Figure 4-2. Plan for Cranking the Car whirligig.

34

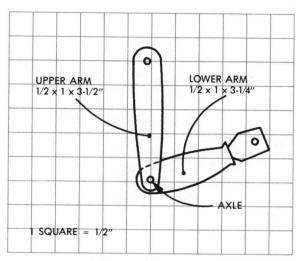

UPPER ARM
1/2 x 1 x 3-1/2"

LOWER ARM
1/2 x 1 x 3-1/4"

AXLE

1 SQUARE = 1/2"

Figure 4-3. Arm detail.

tach a connecting rod between the torso and the cam. Check the movement to make sure all parts work freely.

8. Make a propeller, drilled in the center with a 7/64 in. bit. The best propellers for this whirligig are the cross-lap propeller and the 4-blade Maltese Cross propeller with 6 in. blades. Turn the propeller on the drive shaft with washers in place. You may need a spacer for the drive shaft, but it will not be more than 1/4 in. in length.

9. I painted the automobile black with white tires and yellow spokes, and the gas pump red with a white top with GAS printed on it. The man has blue pants and a yellow shirt. The platform is gray. Of course, you can select your own colors.

Figure 4-4. Baking a Pie whirligig.

Baking a Pie

My wife, Eleanor, has baked hundreds of pies. So when I told her I had run out of ideas for a new whirligig she said, "Why not do a woman rolling dough?" I sat down at the drawing board and drew the design, then built it. This is the Baking a Pie whirligig (Fig. 4-4) that Eleanor inspired.

MATERIALS

Platform: 3/4" x 2-1/4" x 22-1/2"
Extension: 3/4" x 1-1/4" x 4"
Cover: 1/4" x 3/4" x 4"
Table-Legs: (2) 3/4" x 3/4" x 4"
Table Top: 1/2" x 3/4" x 6"

Woman-Leg: 3/4" x 2" x 5"
Torso: 1-1/2" x 3-1/2" x 8"
Arms (2): 1/2" x 1-1/4" x 5-1/2"
Screw Eye Holder: 3/4" x 1/2" x 1-1/4" screw eye
Hip Axle: 1/8" rod, 2" long
Shoulder Axle (2): No. 6 x 1" RHWS
Stove: 1/4" x 5" x 11" plywood
Rolling Pin: see directions and drawing
Pin Axle: 1/8" rod, 2-5/8 " long
Drive Shaft: 1/8" rod, 7-1/2" long, with 1/2" cam
Connecting Rod: 1/16" or 3/32" rod

Tubing: 3/16" brass
Screw Eye: 1/4" or 3/8"
Tension Pin: 3/8" x 2" with cap

PROCEDURE

1. Mark on the platform where holes must be drilled and objects placed as indicated in the drawing. Cut the platform and drill holes to secure the extension (at 2 in.), the pivot socket (at 4-1/2 in.), the screws for the woman's leg (at 6-1/2 in.), and the table legs (at 9-7/8 and 14-1/8 in.) Cut a 1/4 in. slot for the stove back 5-1/4 in. from the rear of the platform (Fig. 4-5).

2. Cut out the platform extension and cut a slot 3/16 in. wide and deep to accommodate the 3/16 in. tubing for the 1/8 in. drive shaft. Attach the extension to the platform with glue and a 1-1/2 in. No. 6 flathead screw. Then glue/brad the cover on. Insert the tension pin with cap in the pivot socket.

3. Make a standard drive shaft with a 1/2 in. cam and insert it in the slot.

4. Cut out the table pieces. Secure the table legs in place with No. 6 flathead screws and glue. Then glue/brad the table top in position. Cut out the stove and fasten it in the slot with brads and glue.

5. Cut out the woman's leg and drill a 3/16 in. hole through the hip point and line it with tubing. Glue/screw the leg in place with the heel about 6 in. from the platform front.

6. Cut out the torso, marking the locations of the shoulder and hip points, then cut out the large slot for the leg (Fig. 4-6). Drill a 3/16 in. hole through the hip and line it with tubing. Drill pilot holes for the shoulder screws that will hold the arms in place. Then shape the body with carving knives (Fig. 4-7). The body should taper slightly toward the front to permit easy movement of the arms. Glue a 3/4 x 1/2 x 1-1/4 in. triangular piece of wood at the bottom end of the skirt to hold the screw eye, then attach the screw eye. Mount the torso on the leg with a 1/8 in. brass rod 2 in. long, threaded 1/8 to 1/4 in. at both ends.

7. Cut out the arms. Drill 3/16 in. holes in the shoulders and insert tubing. Drill 1/8 in. holes in the hands. Then shape the arms with carving knives. Attach the arms to the torso with 3/4 or 1 in. No. 6 brass screws and washers.

8. Make the rolling pin as illustrated (Fig. 4-8). To make the roller, drill a 1-inch piece of 5/8 in. hardwood dowel, with a 3/16 in. bit and line with tubing. Thread a 2-5/8 in. piece of 1/8 in. rod for the pin. Insert the rod in the hands and secure it with 6/32 machine nuts. When the torso is moved forward the arms will push the rolling pin, and when it is moved back, the rolling pin will roll back. The oversized hands will keep the pin on track. Attach the connecting rod, permitting the rolling pin to roll in the middle of the table with the body always leaning forward.

9. The 4-bladed Maltese Cross propellers with either 5 or 6 in. blades work well with this model. If the breezes are insufficient in your area to move the propeller, use the Cross-lap propeller, remembering that a strong wind will

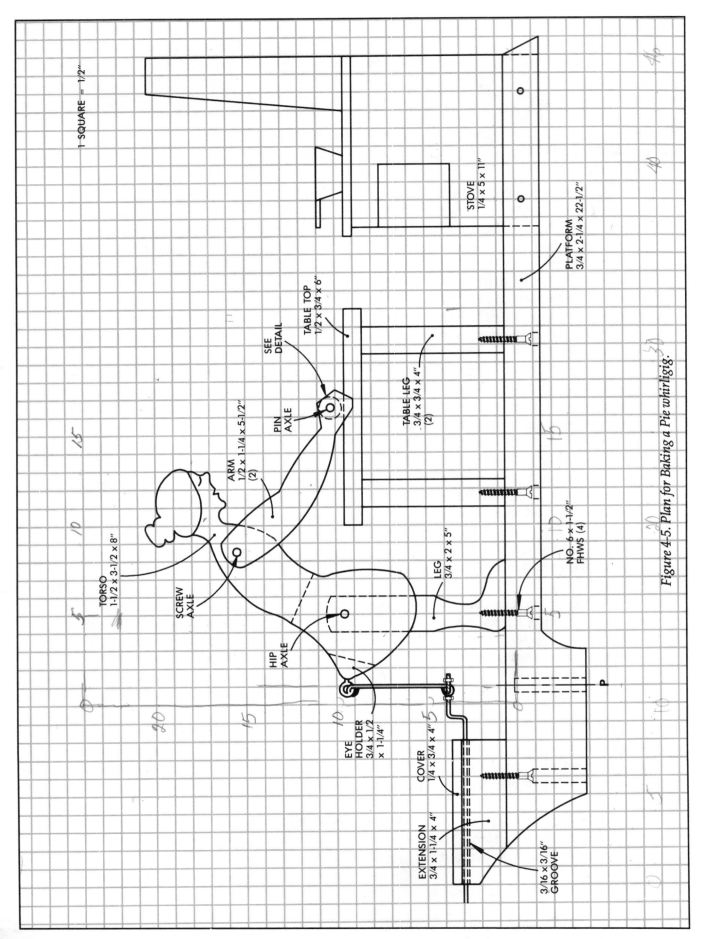

1 SQUARE = 1/2"

STOVE
1/4 x 5 x 11"

PLATFORM
3/4 x 2-1/4 x 22-1/2"

TABLE TOP
1/2 x 3/4 x 6"

SEE
DETAIL

PIN
AXLE

ARM
1/2 x 1-1/4 x 5-1/2"
(2)

TABLE LEG
3/4 x 3/4 x 4"
(2)

TORSO
1-1/2 x 3-1/2 x 8"

SCREW
AXLE

LEG
3/4 x 2 x 5"

NO. 6 x 1-1/2"
FHWS (4)

HIP
AXLE

EYE
HOLDER
3/4 x 1/2
x 1-1/4"

COVER
1/4 x 3/4 x 4"

EXTENSION
3/4 x 1-1/4 x 4"

3/16 x 3/16"
GROOVE

P

Figure 4-5. Plan for Baking a Pie whirligig.

38

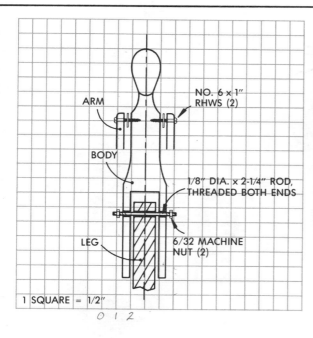

ARM

NO. 6 x 1"
RHWS (2)

BODY

1/8" DIA. x 2-1/4" ROD,
THREADED BOTH ENDS

LEG

6/32 MACHINE
NUT (2)

1 SQUARE = 1/2"

0 1 2

Figure 4-6. Body assembly side view.

make the lady frantically push the rolling pin back and forth across the table.

Figure 4-7. Shaping the body with a carving knife.

10. Paint the platform and the pieces secured to it first. The platform is dull gray, the stove is black with a silver pan, the table is off-white, and the leg is red with yellow stripes. The figure has a white blouse and blue dress with yellow polka dots.

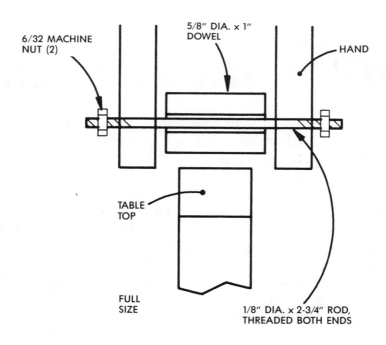

6/32 MACHINE
NUT (2)

5/8" DIA. x 1"
DOWEL

HAND

TABLE
TOP

FULL
SIZE

1/8" DIA. x 2-3/4" ROD,
THREADED BOTH ENDS

Figure 4-8. Rolling pin detail.

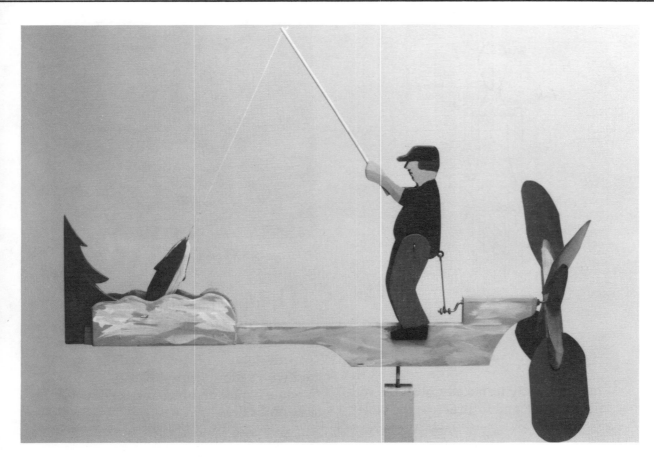

Figure 4-9. First Man/Woman Fishing whirligig.

Man/Woman Fishing

People on whirligigs fish from boats, from the shore, or from the water. Sometimes the boats rock and sometimes the fish is pulled in. In my models the man or woman is standing in the stream. In the first Man/Woman Fishing whirligig (Fig. 4-9), the fisher hauls on the line and a fish emerges from the rapids; this involves a fishing line and movable fish. In the second, the fish is stationary, acting as a rudder to the whirligig, while the fish pole goes up and down (Fig. 4-10). Both are eye-catching.

MATERIALS

Platform: 3/4" x 2-1/4" x 24"
Extension: 3/4" x 1-1/4" x 4"
Cover: 1/4" x 3/4" x 4"
Man-Legs (2): 1/4" x 2-1/4" x 5-7/8"
   Body: 3/4" x 4-1/4" x 6-1/4"
Woman-Legs (2): 1/4" x 2" x 5-3/4"
   Body: 3/4" x 5" x 6-1/4"
Fishing Pole: 3/16" dowel, 11" long

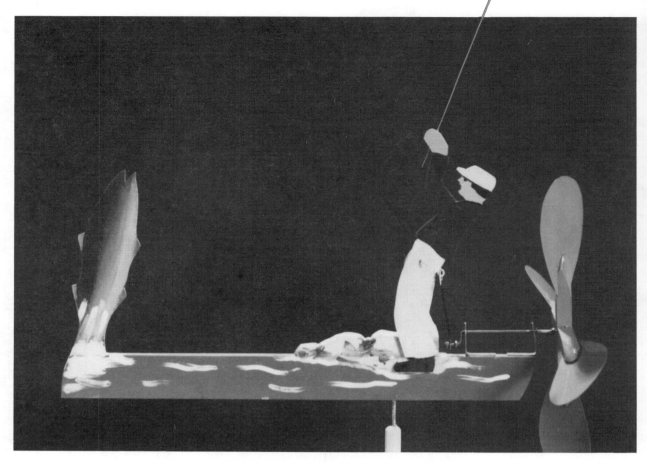

Figure 4-10. Second Man/Woman Fishing whirligig.

Drive Shaft: 1/8" rod, 7-1/2" long,
    with 1/2" cam
Tension Pin: 3/8"diameter, 2"
    long, or other metal liner,
    with cap
Screw Eye: 3/8"
Tubing: 1/8" tubing for hip and
    fish 3/16" tubing for
    extension, 4" long
Axles (2): 3/32" rods for hip and
    fish
Connecting Rod: 1/16" or 3/32"
    rod
First Whirligig
    Tail-Tree: 1/4" x 4" x 7"
    Rapids (2): 1/4" x 3" x 11-1/2"
    Fish: 1/2" x 2-1/4" x 5-1/2"
Second Whirligig
    Fish-Rudder: 1/4" x 3" x 11"

PROCEDURE FOR FIRST WHIRLIGIG

1. Cut out a standard platform and mark the locations of the extension (3 in. from the front), the 1/4 in. tail slot (in 2 in. from the rear), and the rapids pieces (from 12-1/2 in. to the end of the platform). Draw a line 3/4 in. from the top of the platform beginning at 5 in. from the platform front on both sides. This is where the fisherman's shoes will be attached. Drill the pivot socket 6 in. from the front of the platform, line it with tubing, and cap it (Fig. 4-11).

2. Make the extension and attach it with tubing liner and cover.

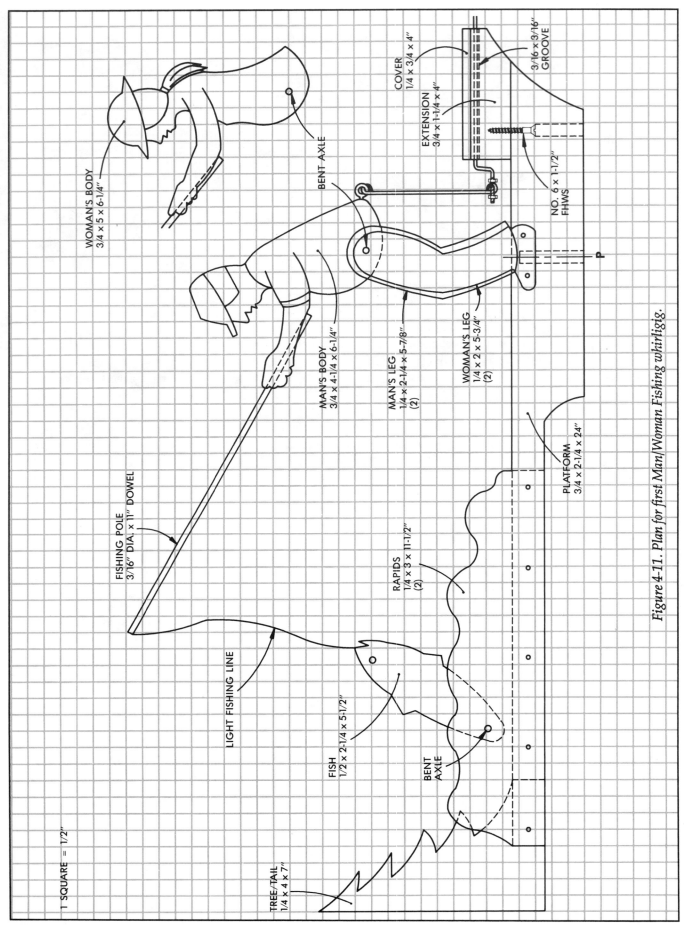

1 SQUARE = 1/2"

WOMAN'S BODY
3/4 x 5 x 6-1/4"

BENT AXLE

COVER
1/4 x 3/4 x 4"

EXTENSION
3/4 x 1-1/4 x 4"

3/16 x 3/16"
GROOVE

NO. 6 x 1-1/2"
FHWS

MAN'S BODY
3/4 x 4-1/4 x 6-1/4"

MAN'S LEG
1/4 x 2-1/4 x 5-7/8"
(2)

WOMAN'S LEG
1/4 x 2 x 5-3/4"
(2)

FISHING POLE
3/16" DIA. x 11" DOWEL

RAPIDS
1/4 x 3 x 11-1/2"
(2)

PLATFORM
3/4 x 2-1/4 x 24"

LIGHT FISHING LINE

FISH
1/2 x 2-1/4 x 5-1/2"

BENT
AXLE

TREE/TAIL
1/4 x 4 x 7"

Figure 4-11. Plan for first Man/Woman Fishing whirligig.

42

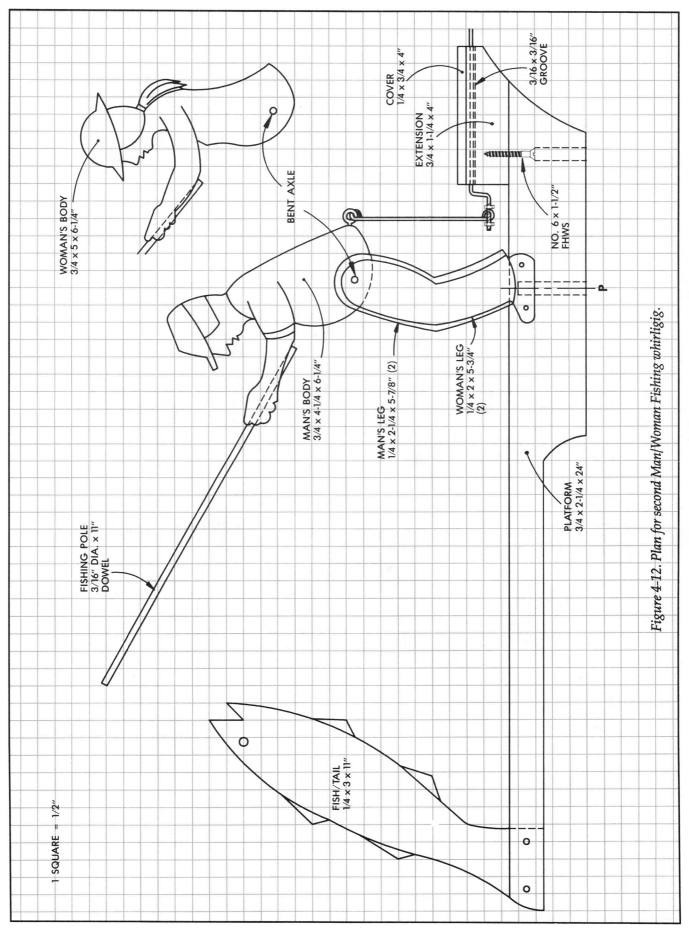

1 SQUARE = 1/2"

WOMAN'S BODY
3/4 x 5 x 6-1/4"

BENT AXLE

COVER
1/4 x 3/4 x 4"

EXTENSION
3/4 x 1-1/4 x 4"

3/16 x 3/16"
GROOVE

NO. 6 x 1-1/2"
FHWS

MAN'S BODY
3/4 x 4-1/4 x 6-1/4"

MAN'S LEG
1/4 x 2-1/4 x 5-7/8" (2)

WOMAN'S LEG
1/4 x 2 x 5-3/4"
(2)

P

FISHING POLE
3/16" DIA. x 11"
DOWEL

PLATFORM
3/4 x 2-1/4 x 24"

FISH/TAIL
1/4 x 3 x 11"

Figure 4-12. Plan for second Man/Woman Fishing whirligig.

43

3. Cut out the tree and the 1/4 in. tail slot and glue/brad the tree in place. Cut out the 2 rapids pieces and glue/brad them in place.

4. Make the drive shaft with a 1/2 in. cam and insert it.

5. Cut out the fisherman's legs, torso, and fishing rod. (Refer to Fig. 4-11 for woman.) Drill a hole for 1/8 in. tubing in the body's hip. The leg hip holes are drilled with a 3/32 in. bit. Attach the legs to the platform with the heels 5 in. from the front. Drill the hands for the 3/16 in. fishing pole. Drill a tiny hole (1/16 in. for the fishing line) 1/4 in. from the end of the pole and insert the pole so that it extends 8-3/4 in. from the hands. Place a screw eye in the bottom rear of the torso. Attach a temporary connecting rod from the screw eye to the drive shaft and check the motion of the fisherman.

6. Make the fish with a 1/8 in. hole 1/2 in. from its tail and insert tubing. Drill a 3/32 in. hole straight across the rapids at a point 3-1/2 in. from the back and 1-3/4 in. from the bottom of the rapids. Suspend the fish by a rod between the rapids pieces. Drill a tiny hole near the fish's mouth for the fishing line.

7. Cut a fish line about 14 in. long from a piece of string, strong thread, or light fishing line. Pass one end through the hole in the fish and secure it with a knot. Pass the other end through the hole in the pole and determine the proper length with the fisher in motion. Do not put a strain on the line because although it may stretch and the pole may bend, the extra strain can cause the propeller to stall.

8. Make and install a 5-inch 4-bladed Maltese Cross propeller.

9. Remove the fish and body to paint them. The platform and attachments can be painted on a stand to resemble a river's colors with blue, green, and white. The rapids pieces are splashed with white. The tree is green. The fisherman's pants are blue jeans, but they could also be yellow or black waders. The shirt and cap are red. The pole may be natural or brown. The fish is the color of your favorite one.

PROCEDURE FOR SECOND WHIRLIGIG

Follow the same procedure as for the first whirligig except for the movable fish, fishing line, and rapids pieces (Fig. 4-12). Only the fisherman with his or her pole will be on the platform. Instead of the tree tail make and insert the large fish rudder (1/4 x 3 x 12 in.). There is no connection between the fishing rod and the rudder. The whirligig is then ready for painting.

Figure 4-13. Fencing the Range whirligig.

Fencing the Range

The Fencing the Range whirligig (Fig. 4-13) scene is familiar to anyone who has put in fence posts or watched it being done. This model is set in the western United States where there are wide ranges to fence in.

MATERIALS

Platform: 3/4" x 2-1/4" x 24"
Drive Shaft: 1/8" rod, 7-1/2" long, with 1/2" cam
Support Brackets: (2) 1-1/2" corner irons
Tail-plywood: 1/4" x 6" x 9"
Workman 1: 3/4" x 4-1/4" x 11"
Post: 1/2" x 1/2" x 7"
Workman 2
    Legs: 1/4" x 2-1/4" x 6"
    Torso: 3/4" x 5" x 7"
Sledge Hammer
    Head: 1/2" x 3/4" x 1-1/2"
    Handle: 1/4" dowel, 4-1/2" long
Socket-Liner: 3/8" Tension Pin, 2" long; cap
Axle: 3/32" brass rod 2-1/2" long,
Tubing: 1/8" brass
Connecting Rod: 1/16" or 3/32" rod
Screw Eye: 1/4" or 3/8"

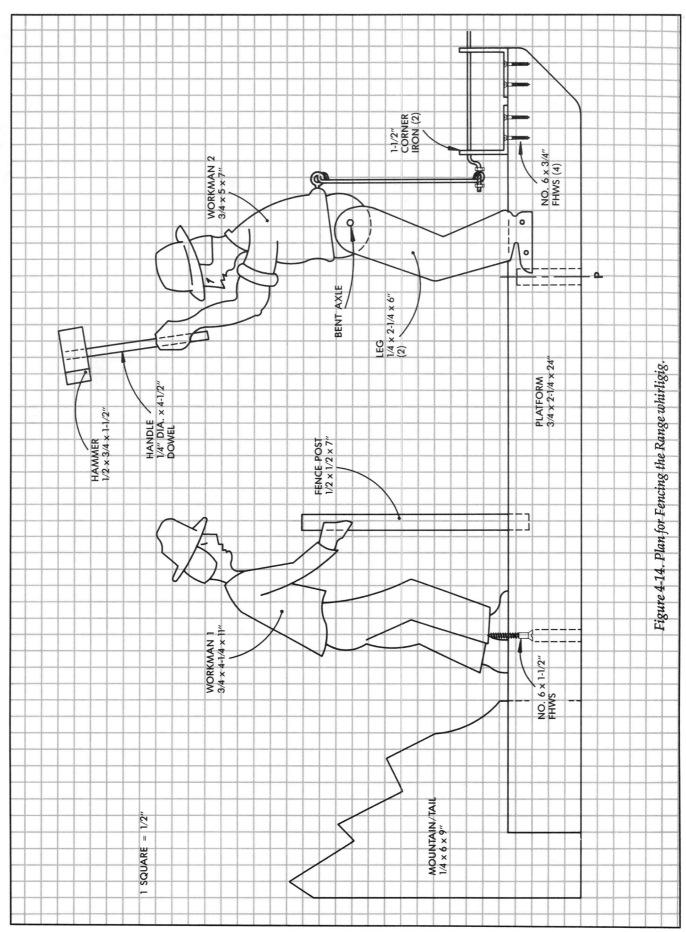

WORKMAN 2
3/4 x 5 x 7"

HAMMER
1/2 x 3/4 x 1-1/2"

HANDLE
1/4" DIA. x 4-1/2"
DOWEL

BENT AXLE

LEG
1/4 x 2-1/4 x 6"
(2)

1-1/2"
CORNER
IRON (2)

NO. 6 x 3/4"
FHWS (4)

P

PLATFORM
3/4 x 2-1/4 x 24"

FENCE POST
1/2 x 1/2 x 7"

WORKMAN 1
3/4 x 4-1/4 x 11"

NO. 6 x 1-1/2"
FHWS

MOUNTAIN/TAIL
1/4 x 6 x 9"

1 SQUARE = 1/2"

Figure 4-14. Plan for Fencing the Range whirligig.

PROCEDURE

1. Make a standard platform, then mark off where the various objects will be located (Fig. 4-14). Cut out the 1/4 in. tail slot 4 in. from the back of the platform. Drill a 3/8 in. pivot socket 7 in. from the front of the platform. Drill a screw hole for the post holder at 18 in. from the front of the platform. Drill a 1/2 in. hole for the post 14-1/2 in. from the front. Draw a line 3/4 in. down from the top edge (from 5 to 7 in. from the front of the platform) where the post driver's shoes will go. Attach the corner irons with the back angle at 3-1/2 in.

2. Make a standard drive shaft. Insert the tension pin and cap, and attach the drive shaft when ready to test the movement.

3. Cut out the remaining parts. Glue/brad the tail in place. Glue and screw the post holder (Workman 1) in position. Glue and screw the post, trimmed to fit the hole 1-2 in. deep. Nail the hands to the post with brads.

4. On Workman 2, drill a 1/8 in. hip hole in the torso and line it with tubing. Drill 3/32 in. hip holes in the legs. Drill the 1/4 in. hammer-handle hole in the hands. Make the hammer, but do not glue the handle to the hands yet. Attach the screw eye to the lower back.

5. Glue/brad the legs of Workman 2 to the platform at the 3/4 in. mark, making sure the holes line up. The heels are 5 in. from the front. Put the torso in place with the axle and washers, then test the movement. Line up the hammer head and the post and glue the hammer to the hands where the position is right.

6. Build the drive shaft and put it in place. Attach the connecting rod, making sure the hammer does not strike the post.

7. Build and attach the propeller. Check the movement. The 16 in. cross-lap propeller works well with this whirligig. The four-bladed Maltese Cross propeller will also operate it in strong breezes.

9. Painting suggestions include blue mountains with snow on the peaks, a sandy yellow platform, and blue jeans for one man and chinos for the other, with red and green shirts.

Figure 4-15. Who's the Boss whirligig.

Who's the Boss?

Who's the Boss (Fig. 4-15) and the Oil Well Pump whirligig show what can be done with movements similar to those used on the Man/Woman Fishing design. If you are designing others like it, keep the relation of the hip axle and the screw eye about the same. This provides for a long movement about the fulcrum, or a bigger swing for the relatively short distance of cam movement.

MATERIALS

Platform: 3/4" x 2-1/4" x 24"
Drive Shaft: 1/8" rod, 7-1/2" long, with 1/2" cam

Support Brackets: (2) 1-1/2" corner irons
Tail: 1/4" x 6" x 9" plywood
Woman-Skirt (2): 3/8" x 2-3/4" x 5-1/2"
   Torso: 3/4" x 5" x 6"
Broom: 1/4" x 1-1/4" x 2"
   Handle: 1/8" dowel, 7-1/2" long
Man: 3/4" x 5" x 10"
Socket Liner: 3/8" tension pin, 2" long; cap
Axle: rod 3/32" x 3" long
Tubing: 1/8" brass tubing
Connecting Rod: 1/16" or 3/32" rod
Screw Eye: 3/8" screw eye

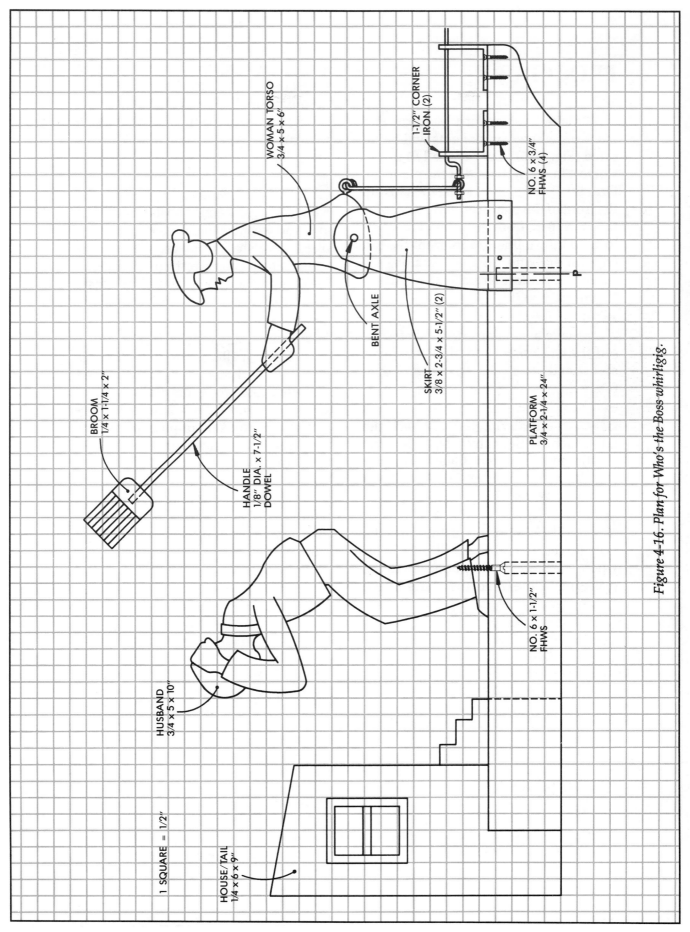

WOMAN TORSO
3/4 x 5 x 6"

1-1/2" CORNER
IRON (2)

NO. 6 x 3/4"
FHWS (4)

P

BENT AXLE

BROOM
1/4 x 1-1/4 x 2"

SKIRT
3/8 x 2-3/4 x 5-1/2" (2)

HANDLE
1/8" DIA. x 7-1/2"
DOWEL

PLATFORM
3/4 x 2-1/4 x 24"

NO. 6 x 1-1/2"
FHWS

HUSBAND
3/4 x 5 x 10"

1 SQUARE = 1/2"

HOUSE/TAIL
1/4 x 6 x 9"

Figure 4-16. Plan for Who's the Boss whirligig.

49

PROCEDURE

1. Make the standard platform and mark off where components will be located (Fig. 4-16). Cut out the 1/4 in. tail slot to 4 in. from the end of the platform. Drill the 3/8 in. pivot socket 7 in. from the front of the platform. Drill a hole for the man 16 in. from the front of the platform. Draw a line 3/4 in. from the top edge for the bottom of the skirt along the side of the platform from 5 to 8 in. Attach the corner irons.

2. Make a standard drive shaft. Insert the tension pin and cap in the pivot socket and attach the drive shaft when ready for it.

3. Cut out all the parts. Attach the tail, which can be of any design. The one illustrated is a house. Glue/screw the man in position with a 1-1/4 in. No. 6 flathead screw.

4. Drill a 3/32 in. hole in the top of the skirt pieces, then drill small pilot holes where the pieces will be attached to the platform. Glue/brad the skirts to the sides of the platform, at 4-3/4 in. from the front. Drill a 1/8 in. hole on the torso for the broom handle in the hands. Drill a 1/8 in. hole in the hip area and line it with tubing. Attach the screw eye to the lower back of the torso.

5. Make the broom and place it in the hands. Put the torso in position with the axle and washers in place. Put the complete drive shaft in place. Attach the connecting rod then test the movement. Make sure the broom comes no closer than 1 to 2 inches of the man's back.

6. Build the propeller. The 16 in. cross-lap propeller is suggested for this whirligig, although both four-bladed Maltese Cross propellers did well. Take your local wind conditions into consideration or make a couple of propellers and test them. Attach the propeller, then check the action.

7. You may want to paint the house white with blue windows. I gave the man a red shirt and blue jeans, and the woman a patterned yellow dress. My platform is green.

Figure 4-17. Oil Well Pump whirligig.

Oil Well Pump

If you've traveled in the West, you've seen oil well pumps, those contraptions that look like giant insects feeding. After one trip, I decided to build a silhouette or two-dimension Oil Well Pump whirligig (Fig. 4-17) that looks much like the ones we saw. The first time I tried, with the help of an engineer, I had to give up because we got involved in the details of the machinery; I was making a miniature pump, not a whirligig. This time I simplified the mechanics and simply kept the form of the moving parts. It is not totally accurate (what whirligig is?), but in silhouette it looks like the real thing. You can make the derrick plain as in the drawing (Fig. 4-18) or you can have oil spouting out.

MATERIALS

Platform: 3/4" x 2-1/4" x 21-1/2"
Extension: 3/4" x 1-3/4" x 4"
Cover: 1/4" x 3/4" x 4"
Tubing: 3/16" x 4" long
Drive Shaft: 1/8" metal rod,
    7-3/4" long, 1" cam
Arm Stand: 3/4" x 2" x 6-1/2"
Pump Arm: 1/4" x 1/2" x 12"
Yoke: 3/4" x 3/4" x 1-1/2"

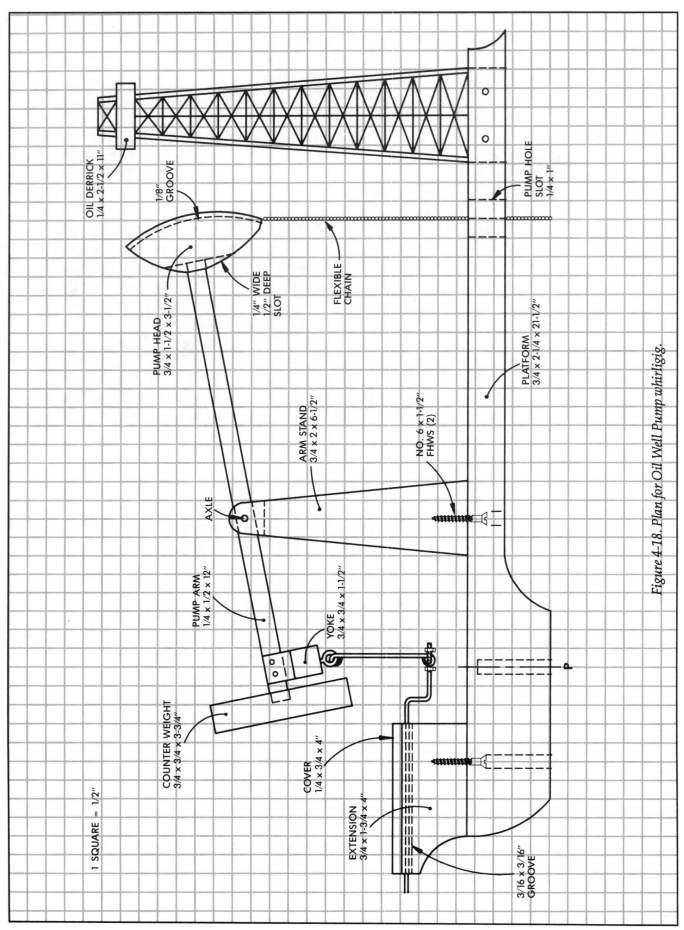

1 SQUARE = 1/2"

OIL DERRICK
1/4 x 2-1/2 x 11"

1/8"
GROOVE

PUMP HEAD
3/4 x 1-1/2 x 3-1/2"

1/4" WIDE
1/2" DEEP
SLOT

FLEXIBLE
CHAIN

PUMP HOLE
SLOT
1/4 x 1"

ARM STAND
3/4 x 2 x 6-1/2"

AXLE

PLATFORM
3/4 x 2-1/4 x 21-1/2"

NO. 6 x 1-1/2"
FHWS (2)

PUMP ARM
1/4 x 1/2 x 12"

COUNTER WEIGHT
3/4 x 3/4 x 3-3/4"

YOKE
3/4 x 3/4 x 1-1/2"

P

COVER
1/4 x 3/4 x 4"

EXTENSION
3/4 x 1-3/4 x 4"

3/16 x 3/16"
GROOVE

Figure 4-18. Plan for Oil Well Pump whirligig.

Pump Head: 3/4" x 1-1/2" x
  3-1/2"
Counterweight: 3/4" x 3/4" x
  3-3/4"
Oil Derrick: 1/4" x 2-1/2" x 11"
Axle: 1/8" rod, 1-1/2" long,
  threaded at ends
Tubing: 3/16" brass
Connecting Rod: 1/16" or 3/32"
  rod
Socket Liner: 3/8" tension pin and
  cap
Screw Eye: 1/4" or 3/8"

PROCEDURE

1. Cut out the platform to the above dimensions. Then mark screw holes for the drive shaft extension (2 in. from the front of the platform), the pivot socket (4-1/2 in. from the front), and the pump stand (8-1/2 in. from the front). Mark the location of the 1/4 in. x 1 in. pump hole slot between 4-1/2 in. and 5-1/2 in. from the rear or derrick-end. Mark the 1/4 in. slot for the derrick-tail extending 3-1/2 in. from the rear.

2. Drill the holes and cut out the slots on the platform. Insert the 2 in. tension pin in the pivot socket with a cap. Cut out the drive shaft extension and make a 3/16" in. slot along the top for the 1/8 in. drive shaft. Glue/brad the cover over the tubing. Cut out the derrick, then glue/brad it in place.

3. Make a special drive shaft from 1/8 in. rod, 7-3/4 in. long and threaded at both ends. The cam or offset should be 1 in. deep. Insert the shaft into the tube and keep it in place with 6/32 in. machine nuts.

4. Next, cut out the arm stand. Cut a 1/4 in. slot 1 in. deep at the top. Then drill a 1/8 in. hole 1/2 in. from the top to hold the arm. Glue/screw the stand in place on the platform.

5. Cut out the pump arm and drill a 3/16 in. hole centered 5 in. from the front. Insert a piece of tubing to prevent wear. Cut out and attach the yoke 3/4 in. from the front and install a screw eye on the bottom (Fig. 4-19). Cut out the

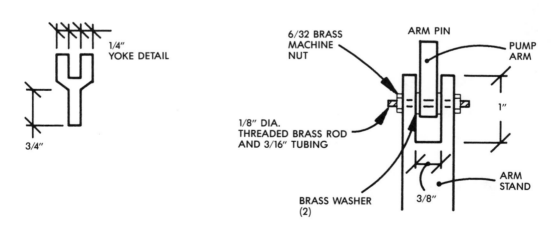

Figure 4-19. Oil Well Pump whirligig detail.

large pump head piece and make a 1/4 in. slot 1/2 in. deep in it for the arm. Glue/brad it on the long arm end.

6. Cut out the counterweight, make a 1/4 in. slot in it, and secure it to the end of the arm. Mount the arm on the stand with a 1/8 in. rod 1-1/2 in. long. This rod, threaded for about 1/4 in. at each end and secured with 6/32 machine nuts and washers, will serve as an axle (Fig. 4-19). Because the arm will be heavier at its long end, shave or file the pump head until it almost balances with the counter-weight. A slight downward pull on the pump head end is desirable.

7. Attach the connecting rod to the screw eye in the yoke when the drive shaft is in mid-position. If the arm wobbles when in motion insert washers at the axle to hold the arm straight. At the large end, attach a flexible rod or chain to pass down through the pump hole in the platform. One end of an inexpensive chain purchased at a jewelry counter can be tacked to the top of the head and hung vertically down through the hole.

8. Make and install the propeller. The best propellers for the Oil Well Pump whirligig are the 4-bladed straight-bladed propeller with 5 in. blades and the 2-bladed Maltese Cross propeller with 6 in. blades. This mechanism moves easily and does not require a large or powerful propeller.

9. A cut-out man or oil crew can be added for a touch of realism. They should be about 5 in. high; if you want the rig to look gigantic, make them 3 in. tall.

10. Paint the platform brown, the platform extension, arm stand and derrick blue. The pump and derrick cap are silver. The derrick and stand struts are black. You can add green grass.

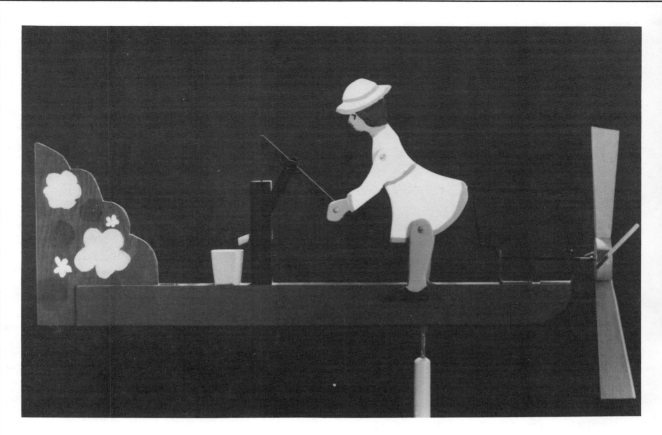

Figure 4-20. Girl at the Pump whirligig.

Girl at the Pump

The woman at the well idea has taken many forms, the most popular is the Girl at the Pump whirligig (Fig. 4-20).

MATERIALS

Platform: 3/4" x 2-1/4" x 24"
Drive Shaft: 1/8" rod, 7-1/2" long, with 1/2" cam
Support Brackets: (2) 1-1/2" corner irons
Socket Liner: 3/8" tension pin, 2" long; cap
Tail: 1/4" x 6" x 9" plywood
Girl-Legs (2): 3/8" x 2" x 4"
    Spacer: 3/4" x 1" x 1"
Body: 3/4" x 5" x 8-1/2"
    Arms (2): 1/4" x 1-1/2" x 4-1/2"
Pump-Casing: 3/4" x 1" x 5"
    Side Frame (2): 1/4" x 1/2" x 4"
    Handle: 1/4" x 1/2" x 5-1/4"
    Piston: any small rod or wire
    Spout: 3/8" dowel, 1" long
    Pail: 3/4" x 1-1/2" x 1-1/2"
Socket Liner: 3/8" tension pin, 2" long; cap
Axles-
    Hip/Shoulder: 1/8" rod, 2-1/8" long, threaded 3/16" to 1/4 in. at both ends, and with 6/32 machine nuts

Hand: 4/44 machine screw 1-1/4"
   long with nuts, or 3/32"
   rod, 2-1/2" long
Pump: 4/44 machine screw
   1-1/2" long with nuts, or
   3/32" rod, 2-1/2" long
Tubing: 3/16" brass
Connecting Rod: 1/16" or 3/32"
   rod
Screw Eye: 1/4" or 3/8"

PROCEDURE

1. Construct the platform and mark off where objects will be located (Fig. 4-21). Cut out the 1/4 in. slot for the tail to 4 in. from the back of the platform. Drill the 3/8 in. pivot socket 7 in. from the front of the platform. Drill a screw hole for the pump 15 in. from the front. Draw a line alongside the platform 3/4 in. from the top edge from 6 to 9 in. from the front. Cut out the tail and glue/brad it in place. Attach the corner irons.

2. Make a standard drive shaft. Insert the tension pin, or other metal liner for the pivot socket, with a cap.

3. Cut out the parts for the girl. In the body drill 3/16 in. holes through the shoulder and hip positions, lining them with tubing. Trim down the front of the body to permit free movement of the arms. Attach the screw eye. Drill 1/8 in. holes in the hands. Glue/brad the legs in place at the 3/4 in. mark with the heels 6-3/4 in. from the front. Drill 1/8" in. holes through the legs making sure the hip holes line up. Glue/brad the spacer in place between the legs. Then put the body in position with the hip axle. Attach the arms to the body.

4. Cut out the pump parts. Drill a 1/4 in. hole in the top of the pump casing 1-1/2 in. deep for the pump piston. Drill a 3/8 in. hole for the spout at 2-1/4 in. from the base. Drill 1/8 in. holes in the pump handle and the side frame pieces. Attach the side pieces to the pump casing as shown in the diagram; the lower edges are 2-1/4 in. from the top of the casing and the upper edges are 5/8 in. from the top. Be sure the holes line up. Glue the spout in place. Screw the pump casing down with glue with the front edge 14-1/2 in. from the front of the platform. Glue the pail in position on the platform, under the spout.

5. Attach the girl's hands to the pump handle with the 4/44 machine screw 1-1/4 in. long. Bend a small rod or wire into the top of the pump handle and insert it into the top of the casing. Attach the pump handle to the side frames with a 4/44 machine screw 1-1/2 in. long. Check the entire movement. As the body moves back and forth the pump handle should go up and down and the piston with it.

6. Put the complete drive shaft in position. Attach the connecting rod.

7. Build the propeller and see how the wind moves it. The shorter (5 in. four-bladed) Maltese Cross propeller is satisfactory for this whirligig.

8. Consider painting the platform green, the girl's dress yellow with a flowered pattern, and the pump gray or black. Paint varicolored bushes on the tail.

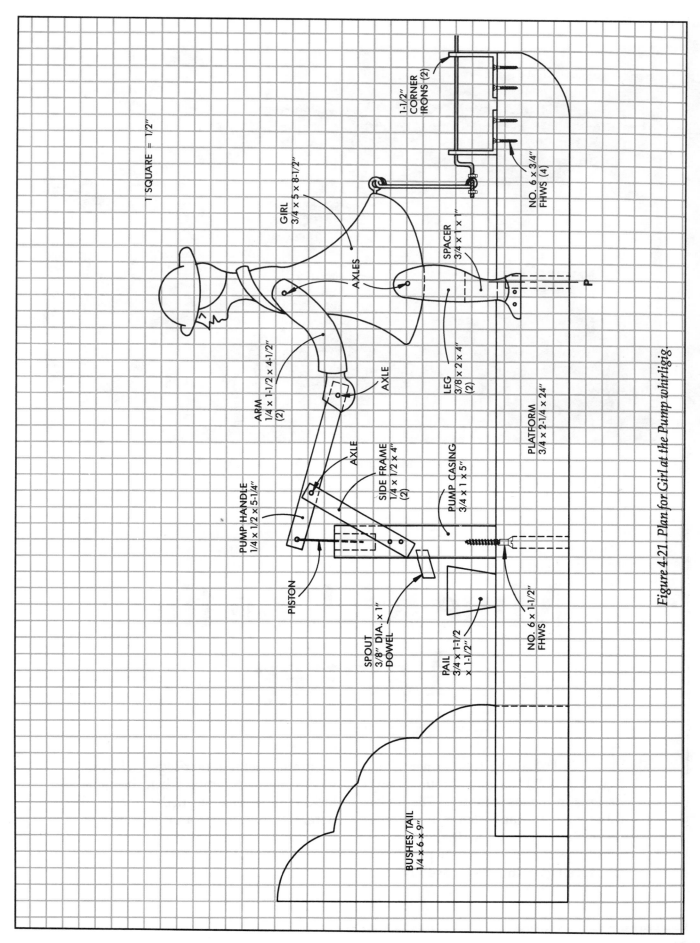

1 SQUARE = 1/2"

GIRL
3/4 x 5 x 8-1/2"

AXLES

SPACER
3/4 x 1 x 1"

LEG
3/8 x 2 x 4"
(2)

ARM
1/4 x 1-1/2 x 4-1/2"
(2)

AXLE

AXLE

SIDE FRAME
1/4 x 1/2 x 4"
(2)

PUMP HANDLE
1/4 x 1/2 x 5-1/4"

PUMP CASING
3/4 x 1 x 5"

PLATFORM
3/4 x 2-1/4 x 24"

PISTON

SPOUT
3/8" DIA. x 1"
DOWEL

PAIL
3/4 x 1-1/2
x 1-1/2"

NO. 6 x 1-1/2"
FHWS

BUSHES/TAIL
1/4 x 6 x 9"

1-1/2"
CORNER
IRONS (2)

NO. 6 x 3/4"
FHWS (4)

P

Figure 4-21 Plan for Girl at the Pump whirligig

Figure 4-22. Mule Kicking the Farmer whirligig.

Mule Kicking the Farmer

The Mule Kicking the Farmer whirligig (Fig. 4-22) has gone through many designs in the last century. The major differences are the location of the connecting rod on the mule. In the simplest whirligigs the mule is in one piece plus the forelegs. In some cases he has separate, kicking rear-legs. On one model the man jumps when the mule kicks him. In the basic model illustrated here, the mule body and legs are one piece, and the farmer doesn't move. Try your own imagination on the design.

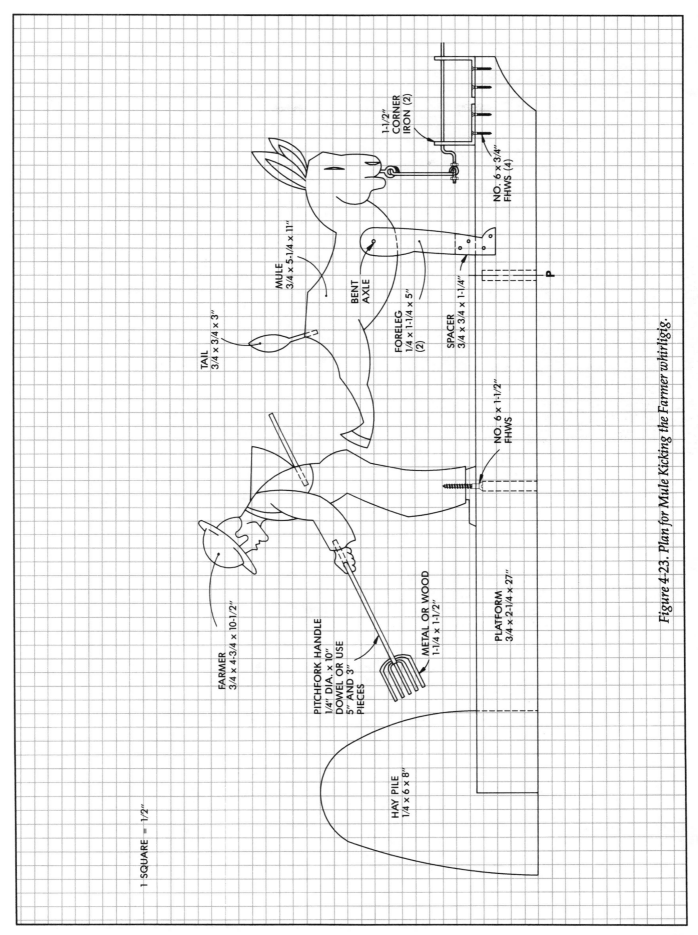

1 SQUARE = 1/2"

TAIL
3/4 x 3/4 x 3"

MULE
3/4 x 5-1/4 x 11"

BENT
AXLE

FORELEG
1/4 x 1-1/4 x 5"
(2)

SPACER
3/4 x 3/4 x 1-1/4"

1-1/2"
CORNER
IRON (2)

NO. 6 x 3/4"
FHWS (4)

P

NO. 6 x 1-1/2"
FHWS

FARMER
3/4 x 4-3/4 x 10-1/2"

PITCHFORK HANDLE
1/4" DIA. x 10"
DOWEL OR USE
5" AND 3"
PIECES

METAL OR WOOD
1-1/4 x 1-1/2"

PLATFORM
3/4 x 2-1/4 x 27"

HAY PILE
1/4 x 6 x 8"

Figure 4-23. Plan for Mule Kicking the Farmer whirligig.

MATERIALS

Platform: 3/4" x 2-1/4" x 27"
Drive Shaft: 1/8" rod, 7-1/2" long,
    with 1/2" cam
Support Brackets (2): 1-1/2"
    corner irons
Mule Body: 3/4" x 5-1/4" x 11"
    Legs (2): 1/4" x 1-1/4" x 5"
    Tail: 3/4" x 3/4" x 3"
    Spacer: 3/4" x 3/4" x 1-1/4"
Farmer: 3/4" x 4-3/4" x 10-1/2"
Pitch Fork Handle: 1/4" dowel,
    10" long, or use 5" and 3"
    pieces
    Tines: 1/1-4" x 1-1/2" metal or
    wood
Hay Pile: 1/4" x 6" x 8"
Socket Liner: 3/8" tension pin, 2"
    long; cap
Axle: 3/32 rod, 3" long
Tubing: 1/8" tubing
Connecting Rod: 1/16" or 3/32"
    rod
Screw Eye: 1/4" or 3/8"

PROCEDURE

1. Make the longer-than-usual platform using the above dimensions, then mark where objects will be located (Fig. 4-23). Make a 1/4 in. slot for the tail in 3 in. from the end. Drill the 3/8 in. pivot socket 8 in. from the front. Drill the screw hole for the farmer 15-3/4 in. from the front. Draw a line 3/4 in. from the top edge for the mule's front leg along the side of the platform from 6 to 8 in. from the front. Attach the corner irons.

2. Make a standard drive shaft. Insert the tension pin and cap in the pivot socket.

3. Cut out the hay pile tail and glue/brad it in the tail slot.

4. Cut out the mule. Drill a 1/8 in. hole in the mule's body where the legs will be, then line it with tubing. Put the screw eye into the mule's nose. Cut out the mule's legs and drill a 3/32 in. hole 1/2 in. from the top of the legs for the axle. Glue/screw the legs onto the side of the platform 6-1/4 in. from the front, making sure the holes are even. Hold the mule in position so that his head swings over the cam. Glue/brad the support spacer in place so it does not bind the action.

5. Hold the farmer in position on the platform with the heel of his shoe about 15 in. from the front. The mule should kick without actually striking the farmer. Drill a 1/4 in. hole into his body and glue the pitch fork into position. Then glue/screw the farmer into place.

6. Assemble all the parts. Install the complete drive shaft. Install the mule body with axle and washers. Attach the connecting rod, then make final adjustments of the mechanism.

7. Then build and attach the propeller. The 16 in. cross-lap propeller works best with this model. If the winds in your area are continuously strong, one of the four-bladed Maltese Cross propellers should be used. Check the movement.

8. Paint the farmer's shirt red and his overalls blue. Give him a yellow straw hat. Paint the mule gray with a whitish face and lower legs. The hay pile may be yellow and the platform green.

Figure 4-24. Pecking Woodpecker whirligig.

Pecking Woodpecker

The red-headed woodpecker (Melanerpes erythrocephalus) is not as numerous in the Eastern United States as formerly, but his pneumatic bill is still busy on whirligigs. This Pecking Woodpecker whirligig (Fig. 4-24) operates with a 3/4 in. cam. If you want the bird to have a longer reach, increase the cam to 1 inch and cut a 1-1/2 in. chunk out of the platform 1/2 in. deep to make room for it.

MATERIALS

Platform: 3/4" x 2-1/4" x 21-1/2"

Drive Shaft: 1/8" rod, 7-1/2" long, with 3/4" cam
Support Brackets: (2) 1-1/2" corner irons
Tree: 1/4" x 10-1/2" x 16-1/2" plywood
Bird: 3/4" x 4" x 12"
    Legs (2): 1/2" x 1" x 6"
    Spacer: 3/4" x 1" x 2"
Reinforcement (2): 1/16" x 3/4" x 2"
Socket Liner: 3/8" Tension Pin, 2" long; cap
Axle: 1/8" brass rod, 2" long, threaded 3/16" or 1/4" at

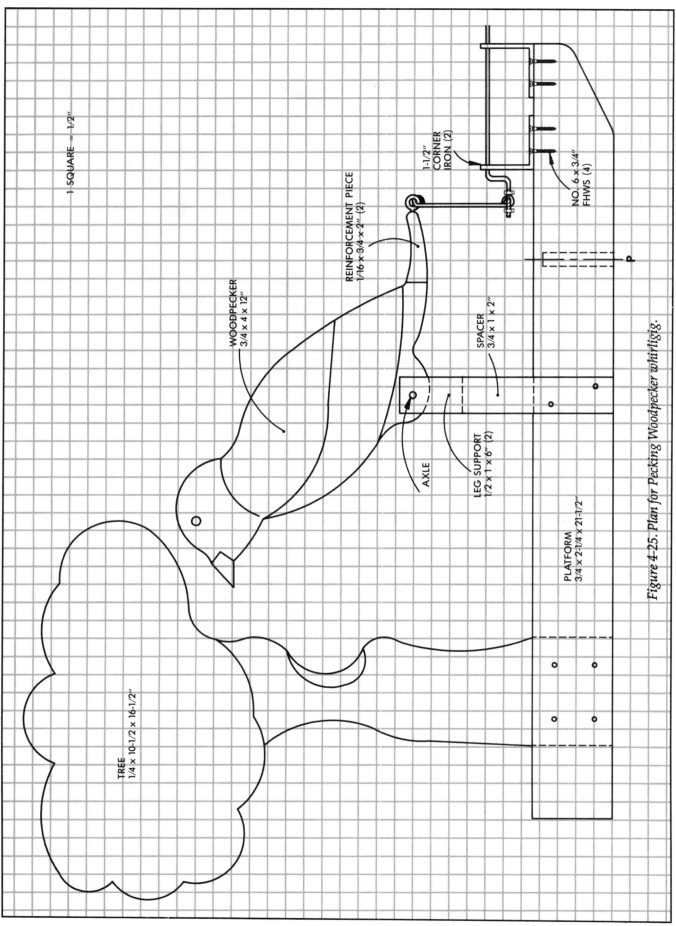

1 SQUARE = 1/2"

WOODPECKER
3/4 x 4 x 12"

REINFORCEMENT PIECE
1/16 x 3/4 x 2" (2)

1-1/2"
CORNER
IRON (2)

NO. 6 x 3/4"
FHWS (4)

SPACER
3/4 x 1 x 2"

AXLE

LEG SUPPORT
1/2 x 1 x 6" (2)

PLATFORM
3/4 x 2-1/4 x 21-1/2"

TREE
1/4 x 10-1/2 x 16-1/2"

P

Figure 4-25. Plan for Pecking Woodpecker whirligig.

both ends, with 6/32 machine nuts

Tubing: 3/16" brass

Connecting Rod: 1/16" or 3/32" rod

Screw Eye: 1/4" or 3/8"

PROCEDURE

1. Make the platform and mark off where objects will be located (Fig. 4-25). Drill the pivot socket 6 in. from the front. Cut a 1/4 in. tail slot to 5 in. from the back. Attach the corner irons and make a standard drive shaft. Insert the tension pin and cap.

2. Cut out the legs. Drill a 1/8 in. hole in the legs 1/2 in. from the top. Glue/brad the legs 9-1/4 in. from the front end, making sure the holes line up. A support spacer can be placed between the legs for greater strength.

3. Cut out the woodpecker. Drill a 3/16 in. hole near the bird's feet as indicated. Line it with tubing. Glue reinforcement pieces on the sides so the tail won't break off or split when the screw eye is attached. Then drill a pilot hole for the screw eye. Place a screw eye at the end of the bird's tail. Position the bird with the axle and washers.

4. Cut out the tree. Place it temporarily in the tail slot and test the bird's back-and-forth movement. The head should fit into the cut in the tree trunk. Then glue/brad the tree in place.

5. Build the drive shaft and place it in position. Attach the connecting rod. Its length will be determined by the place where the head stops at the tree cut. The beak should approach the cut but not strike it.

6. Make and attach the propeller. The 16 in. cross-lap propeller is used with this whirligig. If strong local winds prevail, try the 4-bladed Maltese Cross propellers. Check the total action.

7. Colors for the woodpecker are standard: red head, black wings and white body. The tree trunk is brown, the cut yellow, and the leaves green. The platform can also be green.

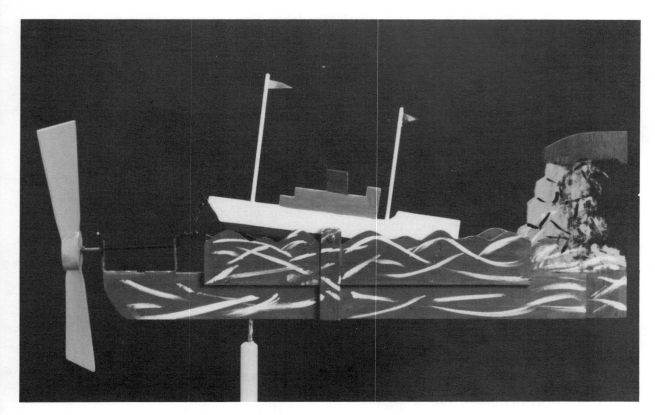

Figure 4-26. Ship on the Rocks whirligig.

Ship on the Rocks

This Ship on the Rocks whirligig (Fig. 4-26) shows a ship in heavy seas, wind behind her, headed for certain doom on a rocky cliff.

MATERIALS

Platform: 3/4" x 2-1/4" x 23"
Drive Shaft: 1/8" rod, 7-1/2" long, with 1/2" cam
Support Brackets: (2) 1-1/2" corner irons
Rock Cliff-plywood: 1/4" x 6" x 9"
Side Supports: (2) 1/2" x 1" x 4-1/2"
Ship: 3/4" x 3-1/2" x 12"
Masts (2): 3/16 dowel, 6-1/2" long

Side Strips (4): (2) 1/8" x 1/2" x 5-1/2"
(2) 1/8" x 1/2" x 9"
Wave Pieces (4): (2) 1/4" x 2-1/2" x 5-1/2"
(2) 1/4" x 2-1/2" x 9"
Socket Liner: 3/8" tension pin, 2" long; cap
Axle: 1/8" rod, 2-1/2" long, threaded 3/16" on both ends, and with 6/32 machine nuts
Tubing: 3/16" brass
Connecting Rod: 1/16" or 3/32" rod
Screw Eye: 1/4" or 3/8"

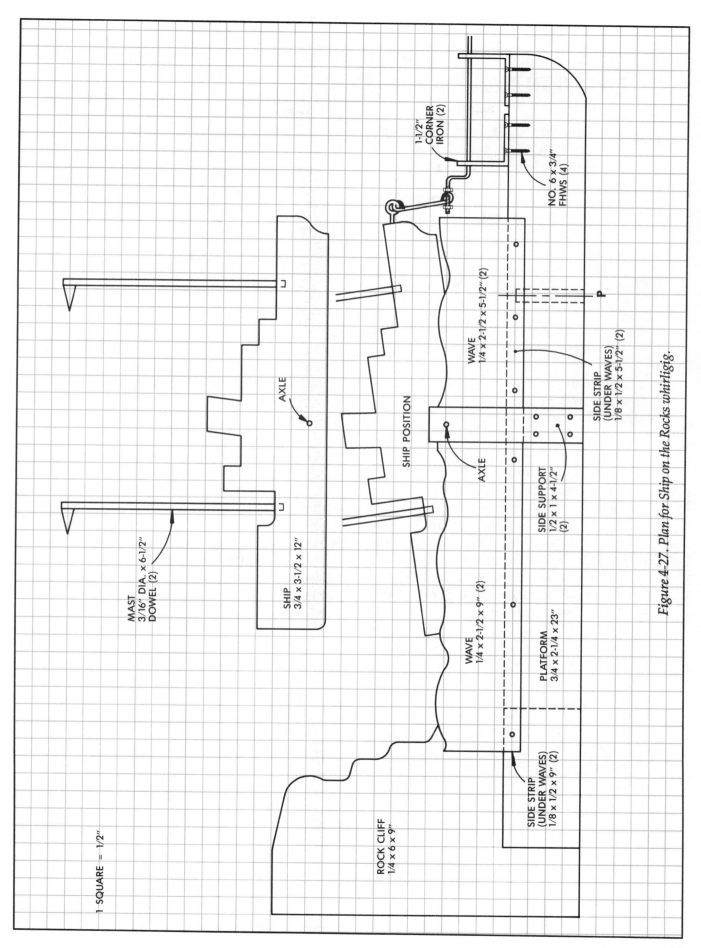

1 SQUARE = 1/2"

MAST
3/16" DIA. x 6-1/2"
DOWEL (2)

AXLE

SHIP
3/4 x 3-1/2 x 12"

SHIP POSITION

AXLE

WAVE
1/4 x 2-1/2 x 5-1/2" (2)

SIDE STRIP
(UNDER WAVES)
1/8 x 1/2 x 5-1/2" (2)

P

SIDE SUPPORT
1/2 x 1 x 4-1/2"
(2)

WAVE
1/4 x 2-1/2 x 9" (2)

PLATFORM
3/4 x 2-1/4 x 23"

1-1/2"
CORNER
IRON (2)

NO. 6 x 3/4"
FHWS (4)

ROCK CLIFF
1/4 x 6 x 9"

SIDE STRIP
(UNDER WAVES)
1/8 x 1/2 x 9" (2)

Figure 4-27. Plan for Ship on the Rocks whirligig.

PROCEDURE

1. Cut out the platform 1 in. shorter than standard (Fig. 4-27). Then mark where the objects will be located. Cut the 1/4 in. slot for the tail to 4 in. from the rear of the platform. Drill a 3/8 in. hole for the pivot socket 7 in. from the front. Cut out the tail and glue/brad it in place. Insert the tension pin or metal liner and cap in the pivot socket. Attach the corner irons.

2. Make a standard drive shaft. Attach the drive shaft when ready.

3. Cut out the side supports and drill a 1/8 in. hole 1/2 in. from the top ends. The side supports are centered 10-1/4 to 11-1/4 in. from the front, which places the hole at about 1-3/4 in. above the platform. Glue/brad the side supports in place, making sure the holes are even.

4. Cut out the boat and drill 3/16 in. holes for the masts. Drill a 3/16 in. hole at the middle of the boat 1/2 in. from the bottom, and insert brass tubing. Test the boat rocking on the side supports with a 1/8 in. brass rod as axle.

5. Glue/brad the side strips in place along the top of the platform. For the waves, mark off 1/2 in. along the top of the wave pieces. Do not cut below this mark when cutting out the wave curves; otherwise too much of the hull will be exposed. Glue/brad the wave pieces in place over the side strips to give free play to the ship. If the wave pieces bind the ship's movement, tack 1 or 1-1/4 in. blocks (1/4 x 1/2 x 1 in.) between the wave pieces near the stern of the ship on one end and near the rocks on the other.

6. Mount the ship on the axle between the side supports, with washers in place. The threaded axle is held in position with 6/32 machine nuts.

7. Make and attach the propeller. Either one of the two-bladed Maltese Cross propellers is suitable for this whirligig because the boat is in excellent balance. Check the movement.

8. Paint the hull black, the superstructure white, the platform blue-green, and the waves blue-green with white tops. Make the shore rocks gray with a green top.

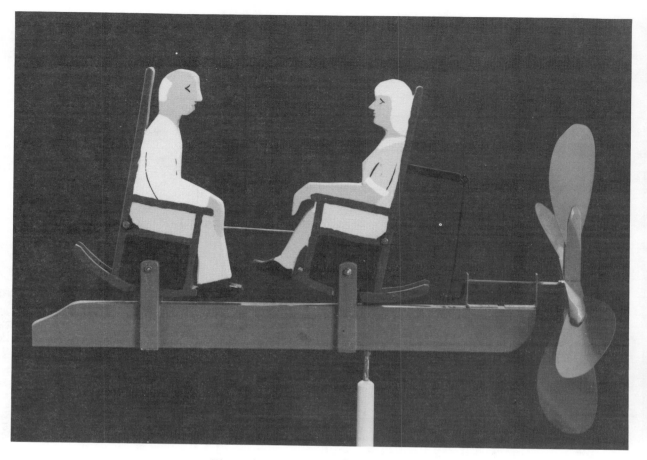

Figure 4-28. Ol' Rockin' Chair whirligig.

Ol' Rockin' Chair

The Ol' Rockin' Chair whirligig (Fig. 4-28) represents leisure, retirement, or mild exercise. I had no trouble making one chair rock but couldn't make two rock without an extended drive shaft and two cams. For this model, I synchronized the movements of the chairs with a connecting rod so that the rocking action of one chair moves the other. The only trouble is that they move in the same direction, and never toward each other.

MATERIALS

Platform: 3/4"x 2-1/4" x 24"
Drive Shaft: 1/8" rod, 7-1/2" long, with 1/2" cam
Support Brackets: (2) 1-1/2" corner irons
Rocking Chair
  Man: 3/4" x 6-1/4" x 11"
  Woman: 3/4" x 6-1/4" x 10-3/4"
Additional Rockers (4): 3/16" x 3/8" x 3"

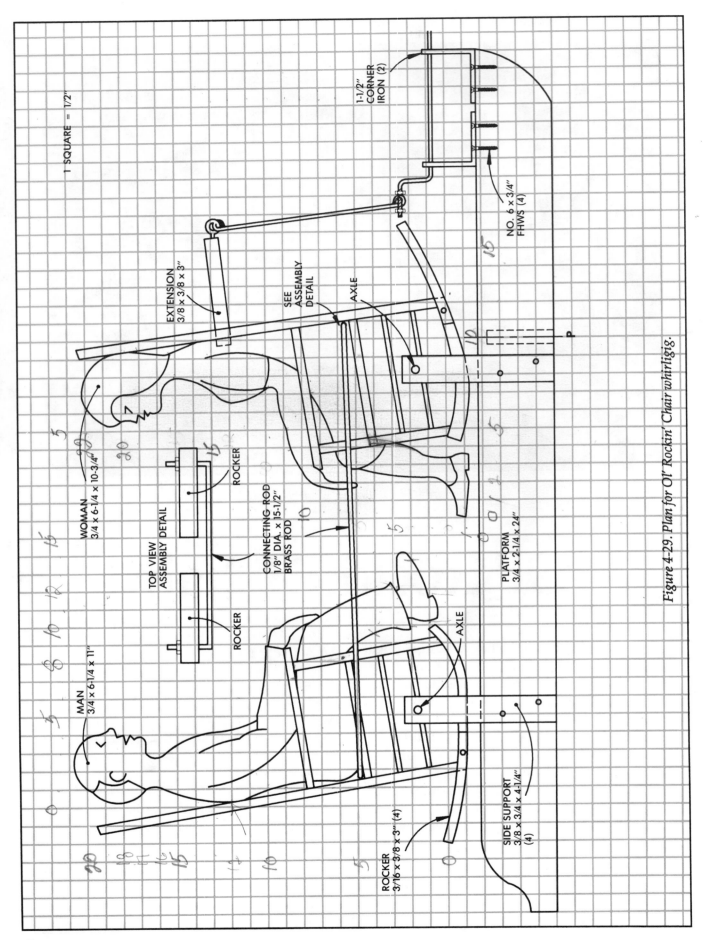

1 SQUARE = 1/2"

EXTENSION
3/8 x 3/8 x 3"

1-1/2"
CORNER
IRON (2)

NO. 6 x 3/4"
FHWS (4)

SEE
ASSEMBLY
DETAIL

AXLE

P

WOMAN
3/4 x 6-1/4 x 10-3/4"

ROCKER

TOP VIEW
ASSEMBLY DETAIL

CONNECTING ROD
1/8" DIA. x 15-1/2"
BRASS ROD

ROCKER

PLATFORM
3/4 x 2-1/4 x 24"

MAN
3/4 x 6-1/4 x 11"

AXLE

SIDE SUPPORT
3/8 x 3/4 x 4-1/4"
(4)

ROCKER
3/16 x 3/8 x 3" (4)

Figure 4-29. Plan for Ol' Rockin' Chair whirligig.

Chair/Side Supports: (4) 3/8" x
 3/4" x 4-1/4"
Chair Extension: 3/8" x 3/8" x 3"
Rocker Connecting Rod: 1/8"
 brass rod, 15-1/2" long
Socket Liner: 3/8" tension pin, 2"
 long; cap
Axles (2): 1/8" brass rod, 2-1/8"
 long, threaded with 6/32
 machine nuts
Tubing: 3/16" tubing for liners
Connecting Rod: 3/32" rod
Screw Eye: 3/8"

PROCEDURE

1. Make the standard platform and mark off where objects will be located (Fig. 4-29). Drill the 3/8 in. hole for the pivot socket 8 in. from the front of the platform. Attach the corner irons.

2. Make a standard drive shaft. Insert the tension pin or metal liner and cap in the pivot socket. Attach the drive shaft when ready.

3. Cut out the man and woman rockers in their chairs. Drill a 3/16 in. hole where the side support axles will be located, approximately 1-3/4 in. from the backs of the rockers and 1-3/8 in. from the bottom. Drill a 1/8 in. hole for the long 1/8 in. connecting rod where the seat and the rocker back meet, approximately 3/8 in. from the back and 3 in. from the bottom of the rockers. Drill a 3/8 in. hole in the back of the woman's rocker 4-1/4 in. from the top for the chair extension. Cut out the rocker extension and glue it into the hole. Turn a 3/8 in.

screw eye into the end of that piece. Cut out the rocker pieces and glue/brad them on the bottom of the chairs.

4. Cut out the side supports and drill them with a 1/8 in. bit 1/2 in. from the top ends. Then glue/brad them in place centered at approximately 9 and 18-1/2 in. from the front of the platform. Make sure the holes are level. Put the chairs in position with the two axles between the support pieces. Test the movement.

5. Fit the long 1/8 in. connecting rod in place on the chairs. Bend one end of the rod at 1-1/2 in. to allow it to penetrate the rocking chair and extend about 1/4 in. on the other side. Then measure where the long rod should be bent on the other end; the straight section between bends should be about 12-1/2 in. Thread the ends of the rods 3/16 in. to 1/4 in. for the 6/32 machine nuts. Test the movement of the chairs with the larger connecting rod in place.

6. Construct and install the drive shaft. Attach the connecting rod to the drive shaft, making sure everything works right.

7. Build and add the propeller. The 16 in. cross-lap propeller is suggested for this whirligig. Check the entire action.

8. Paint the rocking chairs brown or red. Give the man blue trousers and a white shirt. Make the woman a patterned yellow dress. Paint the platform white.

Figure 4-30. Bucking Bronco whirligig.

Bucking Bronco

The Bucking Bronco or Cowboy whirligig (Fig. 4-30), in addition to the drive shaft, has a control wire which makes the hind legs buck as the pony rears its hindquarters. Proper balance is vital to the operation of this whirligig. This may require some experimentation with the location of the hub hole and axle. If the movement is heavy, a larger propeller may be necessary.

MATERIALS

Platform: 3/4" x 2-1/4" x 24"
Drive Shaft: 1/8" rod, 9-1/2" long, with 1/2" cam
Support Bracket: (2) 1-1/2" corner irons
Tail-plywood: 1/4" x 5" x 10"
Cowboy/Bronco: 3/4" x 10" x 12"
Forelegs (2): 3/8" x 1-1/2" x 6"

Spacer: 3/4" x 3/4" x 2-1/2"
  (shaped)
Hind Legs (2): 1/4" x 2-1/2" x 7"
Back pieces: 1/4" x 1-1/2" x 2"
  (shaped)
Pony Tail: 3/8" x 1-1/4" x 5"
  (carved)
Socket Liner: 3/8" tension pin, 2"
  long; cap
Axles (2): 1/8" brass rod, 2-1/4"
  long, threaded 3/16" or
  1/4"at both ends, and
  6/32 machine nuts
Tubing: 3/16" brass
Control wire: 0.039 music wire
  (stiff, 12" long), with 4
  small (1/4") screw eyes
Connecting Rod: 1/16" or 3/32"
  rod
Screw Eye: 3/8"

PROCEDURE

1. Cut out the platform and mark off where the objects will be located (Fig. 4-31). Cut out the 1/4 in. slot for the tail 3 in. back from the end of the platform. Drill the 3/8 in. pivot socket 7 in. from the front. Draw a line 3/4 in. from the top edge of the platform for the hoof location. Attach the corner irons.

2. Make the drive shaft. Insert the tension pin, or metal liner, and cap in the pivot socket. Attach the drive shaft when ready.

3. Cut out the tail. The tail resembles a fence, so it can be scored before being attached. Glue/brad it into the tail slot.

4. Cut out the forelegs and drill a 1/8 in. hole 3/4 in. from the top. Glue/brad them in position, making sure the holes line up. The hooves are 8-1/2 in. from the front of the platform. Turn small (1/4 in.) screw eyes into the backs of the legs at about 2-1/4 in. from the top of the platform.

5. Cut out the pony and rider. Drill two 3/16 in. holes as shown (Fig. 4-31) for the axles through the pony's body and line them with brass tubing. Cut out and shape the pony's tail then drill a 3/8 in. hole and glue it in. Attach the screw eye in the pony's neck. Make the axles and place the pony between the forelegs with washers. Glue/brad in the spacer piece, making sure it does not interfere with the movement of the bronco.

6. Put the completed drive shaft in place and attach the connecting rod.

7. Make the hind legs of 1/4-in. plywood. Glue on the back pieces to hold the legs out from the hindquarters (Fig. 4-32). Drill a 1/8 in. hole through the legs as indicated. Turn small screw eyes (1/4 in.) into the top of the legs. Place the axle through the body with washers and put the legs in position. Secure the axle with nuts at the ends. With the cam in the up position, place each leg at a 45-degree angle and secure a stiff control wire between the screw eyes. Turn the drive shaft. When the pony's head goes down, the hind legs will kick up.

8. Make and install the propeller. The 16 in. cross-lap propeller is recommended for this whirligig. Check the whole action. For added effect, drill small holes in the rider's hands and coil a thin wire through the cowboy's upright hand for a rope. Run another wire from his lower hand to the pony's mouth for reins.

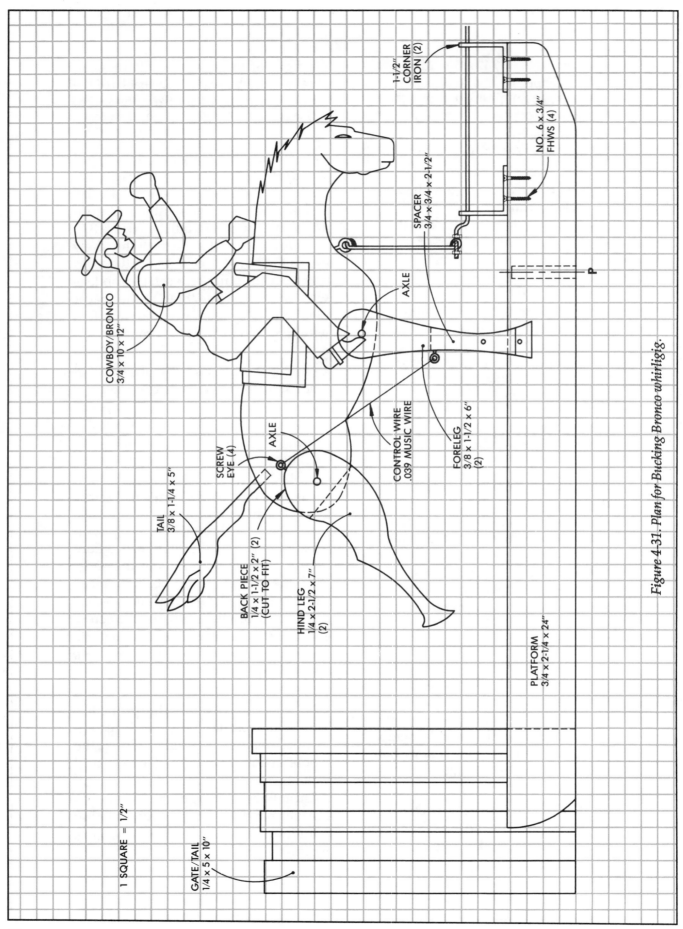

Figure 4-31. Plan for Bucking Bronco whirligig.

COWBOY/BRONCO
3/4 x 10 x 12"

AXLE

1-1/2"
CORNER
IRON (2)

SPACER
3/4 x 3/4 x 2-1/2"

NO. 6 x 3/4"
FHWS (4)

P

AXLE

SCREW
EYE (4)

TAIL
3/8 x 1-1/4 x 5"

BACK PIECE
1/4 x 1-1/2 x 2" (2)
(CUT TO FIT)

HIND LEG
1/4 x 2-1/2 x 7"
(2)

CONTROL WIRE
.039 MUSIC WIRE

FORELEG
3/8 x 1-1/2 x 6"
(2)

PLATFORM
3/4 x 2-1/4 x 24"

1 SQUARE = 1/2"

GATE/TAIL
1/4 x 5 x 10"

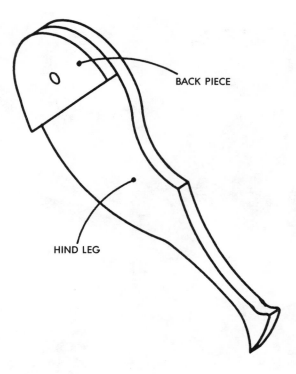

BACK PIECE

HIND LEG

Figure 4-32. Hind leg detail.

9. Paint the bronco white with brown spots. Give the cowboy blue jeans, a tan jacket, and a red shirt. Paint the fence yellow and the platform green.

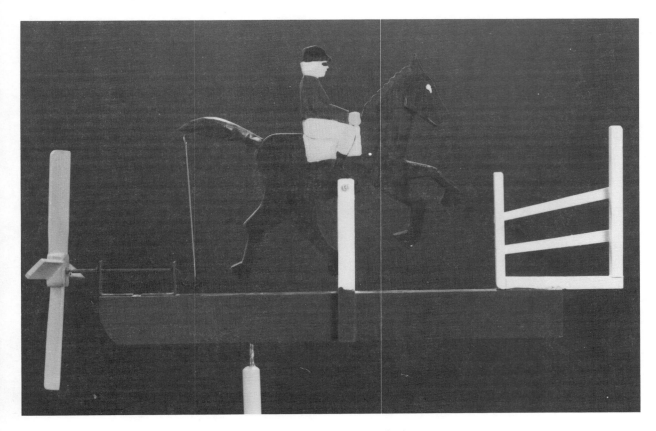

Figure 4-33. Equestrienne whirligig.

Equestrienne

The Equestrienne whirligig (Fig. 4-33), preparing to go over a jump, has almost the same problem of balance that a real horse and rider experience. If you want the horse to make more of a rocking motion, a deeper cam can be made in the drive shaft.

MATERIALS

Platform: 3/4" x 2-1/4" x 22"
Drive Shaft: 1/8" rod, 7-1/2" long, with 1/2" cam
Support Brackets: (2) 1-1/2" corner irons

Horse/Rider: 3/4" x 10-1/2" x 11-1/2"
Horses Tail: 3/4" x 1" x 4-1/4" (carved)
Supports (2): 3/8" x 3/4" x 7-1/2"
Fence Pieces
    Posts (2): 1/2" x 1/2" x 6"
        1/2" x 1/2" x 7"
    Boards(2): 1/8" x 1/2" x 6"
    Base: 1/2" x 1/2" x 5-1/2"
Socket Liner: 3/8" tension pin, 2" long
Axle: 1/8" brass rod, threaded 3/16" each end, and 6/32 machine nuts
Tubing: 3/26" brass

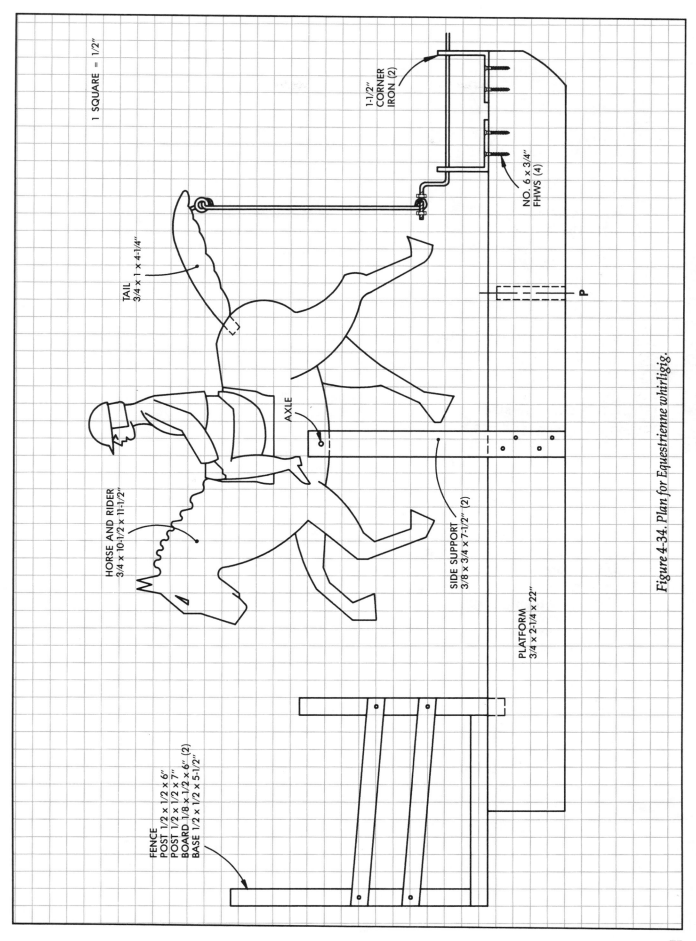

1 SQUARE = 1/2"

1-1/2"
CORNER
IRON (2)

NO. 6 x 3/4"
FHWS (4)

P

TAIL
3/4 x 1 x 4-1/4"

AXLE

HORSE AND RIDER
3/4 x 10-1/2 x 11-1/2"

SIDE SUPPORT
3/8 x 3/4 x 7-1/2" (2)

PLATFORM
3/4 x 2-1/4 x 22"

FENCE
POST 1/2 x 1/2 x 6"
POST 1/2 x 1/2 x 7"
BOARD 1/8 x 1/2 x 6" (2)
BASE 1/2 x 1/2 x 5-1/2"

Figure 4-34. Plan for Equestrienne whirligig.

75

Connecting Rod: 1/16" or 3/32"
rod
Screw Eye: 1/4" or 3/8"

PROCEDURE

1. Cut out the platform and mark where components will be located (Fig. 4-34). Drill a 3/8 in. hole for the pivot socket 7 in. from the front of the platform. Drill a 1/2 in. hole for the tail post 19 in. from the front. Attach the corner irons.

2. Make a standard drive shaft. Insert the tension pin and cap in the socket.

3. Cut out the side supports and drill a 1/8 in. hole 1/2 in. from the top of each support. Nail them in position which will be 11 in. from the front of the platform. Make sure the holes line up.

4. Cut out the horse and rider, then drill a 3/16 in. hole where shown, 1/2 in. up the belly of the horse. Line it with 3/16 in. brass tubing. Drill a 3/4" hole high on the horse's hip for the tail. Carve the tail as shown and glue it in place. Attach the screw eye near the end of the tail. Put the horse with the axle in position between the supports. The best axle is a 1/8 in. rod, about 2-1/4 in. long, threaded 3/16 in. at each end and held in position with 6/32 in. machine nuts. An axle with bent ends can also be used. If the legs strike the side supports, trim them down to fit. Make the front of the horse lighter by trimming the neck and head as needed. If the horse is far off balance, re-drill the holes.

5. Add the connecting rod.

6. Make and add the propeller. The four-bladed straight propeller is best for this whirligig under normal wind conditions. Test the movement. Adjustments may be needed in balancing the horse.

7. Cut out the fence pieces, build the fence, and install it in position.

8. Take the whirligig apart for painting. The rider is formally dressed in black and white, and the horse can be any favorite color. The fence and supports are white and the platform is green.

Figure 4-35. See-Saw whirligig.

See-Saw

The See-Saw whirligig (Fig. 4-35) emulates children playing at a park or school playground. On this whirligig, sink the drive shaft into the platform to reduce the height of the fulcrum on the see-saw board, and to keep the drive shaft out of the way of the children and board (Fig. 4-36).

MATERIALS

Platform: 3/4"x 2-1/8" x 20"
Platform Cover: 1/4" x 3/4" x
   6-1/2"

Drive Shaft: 1/8" steel rod about
   15" long with 1/2" cam
Supports (2): 3/8" x 1"x 5-1/2"
Support Block: 3/4" x 1-3/4" x 2"
See-Saw Board: 1/4" x 3/4" x 14"
Fulcrum: 1/2" x 3/4" x 1"
Boy-Figure: 3/4" x 1-3/4" x 3-1/2"
   Legs (2): 3/4 x 1-1/2" x 3"
Girl-Figure: 3/4" x 2-3/4" x 3"
   Leg A: 3/4" x 1-1/8" x 3-3/4"
   Leg B: 3/4" x 1-1/2" x 3-1/2"
Tail: 1/4" x 5"x 8-1/2" plywood
Socket Liner: 3/8" tension pin, 2"
   long; cap

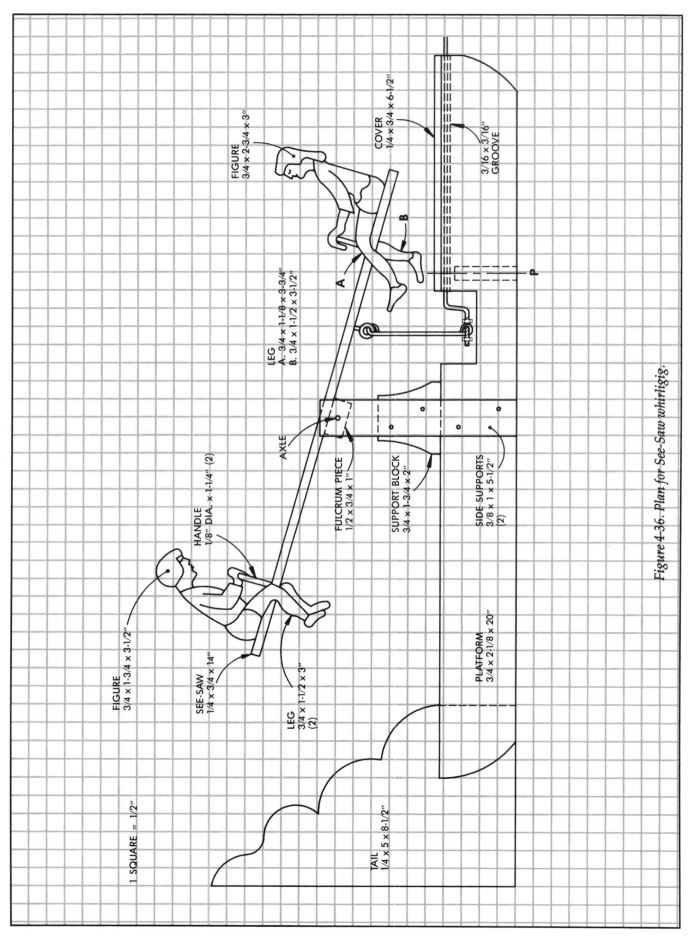

FIGURE
3/4 x 2-3/4 x 3"

COVER
1/4 x 3/4 x 6-1/2"

3/16 x 3/16"
GROOVE

LEG
A. 3/4 x 1-1/8 x 3-3/4"
B. 3/4 x 1-1/2 x 3-1/2"

A

B

P

AXLE

FULCRUM PIECE
1/2 x 3/4 x 1"

SUPPORT BLOCK
3/4 x 1-3/4 x 2"

SIDE SUPPORTS
3/8 x 1 x 5-1/2"
(2)

HANDLE
1/8" DIA. x 1-1/4" (2)

FIGURE
3/4 x 1-3/4 x 3-1/2"

SEE-SAW
1/4 x 3/4 x 14"

LEG
3/4 x 1-1/2 x 3"
(2)

PLATFORM
3/4 x 2-1/8 x 20"

1 SQUARE = 1/2"

TAIL
1/4 x 5 x 8-1/2"

Figure 4-36. Plan for See-Saw whirligig.

78

Axle: 1/8" brass rod, 2-1/8"
long, threaded 3/16"" at
both ends, and 6/32
machine nuts
Tubing: 3/16" brass
Connecting Rod: 3/32" rod
Screw Eye: 3/8"

PROCEDURE

1. Cut out the platform and mark where the components will be located. Cut a 1/4 in. slot for the tail 2 in. into the end. Cut out a 2 in. section of the platform 1 in. deep from 6-1/2 to 8-1/2 in. from the front. At the top of the platform, between the edge and 6-1/2 in. cut a 3/16 in. channel for the drive shaft. Drill a 3/8 in. hole for the pivot socket 6 in. from the front, making sure the channel is not penetrated.

2. Make the drive shaft 10-1/2 in. long including the 1/2 in. cam. It should extend 2 in. beyond the front of the platform. Insert the shaft in the channel with 1 in. long 3/16 in. brass tubing at each end. Glue/brad the cover in position. Cut out the tail and glue/brad it in place.

3. Cut out the side supports and drill a 1/8 in. hole 1/2 in. from the top of each support. Glue/brad them in place, making sure the holes line up. They are located in the middle of the platform; their center is 10 in. from either end.

4. Construct the see-saw board and the fulcrum support. Drill a 3/16 in. hole through the fulcrum and line it with brass tubing. Glue/brad it under the center of the board. Turn the screw eye into the bottom of the board over the cam, about 2-1/2 in. from the center

fulcrum hole. Mount the board on the axle, install the connecting rod and test the action. Glue/brad the support block in position, making sure it does not bind the movement. If it does bind, file down the inside of the side support pieces.

5. Cut out the boy and girl components. Cut, and file or sand the legs to an angle that allows the figures to sit astride the board (Fig. 4-37). A small piece of wood or dowel can be inserted beneath hands which appear to be holding a handle.

6. Make and add the propeller. The four-bladed straight-bladed propeller is adequate for this whirligig. Test the entire movement.

7. Paint the platform and bushes green. Blooms may be painted on the bushes. Paint the children bright colors.

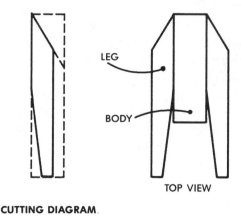

CUTTING DIAGRAM

Figure 4-37. See-Saw whirligig detail.

Figure 4-38. Chickens Feeding whirligig.

Chickens Feeding

The Chickens Feeding whirligig (Fig. 4-38) often portrays a chicken chipping away at an ear of corn. I decided to have two chickens chopping away at piles of grain, using two cams on one shaft. With a longer platform or smaller fowl, three or four chickens can be pecking away by installing more cams into the drive shaft.

MATERIALS

Platform: 3/4"x 2" x 22"
Cover A: 1/4" x 3/4" x 3"
Cover B: 1/4"x 3/4" x 9-1/2"
Rooster: 3/4"x 8" x 11-1/2"
Chicken: 3/4" x 4" x 8-1/2"
Rooster Legs (2): 3/8" x 2" x 4"
Chicken Legs (2): 3/8" x 1" x 3-1/2"
Grain Pile: 3/4" x 3" x 5-1/2"
Tail (large pile): 1/4" x 7-1/2" x 8-1/2"
Socket Liner: 3/8" tension pin, 2" long
Axles (2): 1/8"brass rod, 2-1/8" long, threaded 3/16" at both ends, and 6/32 machine nuts
Tubing: 3/16" brass

Drive Shaft: 1/8" steel rod, 20" long
Connecting Rod: 3/32" rod or stiff wire
Screw Eye: 3/8"

PROCEDURE

1. Cut out the platform and mark where objects will be located (Fig. 4-39). Draw a line 1 in. below the top of the platform for the bottom of the chickens' feet. The chick's feet reach from 5 to 6 in. along the platform and the rooster's from 17-1/2 to 19-1/2 in. Cut a 1/4 in. slot for the tail 2 in. from the back. Cut out two 1 in.-deep sections of the platform, one between 3 and 5 in. from the front and the other between 14-1/2 and 16-1/2 in. Cut out a 3/16 in. channel on the top of the platform from the front of the platform to the second cam cut-out section for the drive shaft.

2. Make the special drive shaft (Fig. 4-40). Thread one end 3/4 in. with a 6/32 die. Then at 1 in. make a 3/4 in. cam. This will be the rear cam for the rooster. **Before proceeding further**, place two 1 in. pieces of 3/16 in. tubing on the shaft; this cannot be done later after more bends are made. At 10-1/2 in. from the first cam, make another 3/4 in. cam for the chicken. As you continue, make sure these bends will fit into the cut-out sections. Cut the drive shaft 2 in. in front of the platform, then thread the end 1 in.

3. Make a spool to carry the connecting rod around the cam by drilling a 3/16-in. hole through a 1/2 x 1/2 x 5/8 in. piece of wood (Fig. 4-41). Then saw it lengthwise and glue the two pieces around a cam, using a small clamp.

When the glue is dry, cut the edges to hold the connecting rod firmly. If you have a motorized jig saw, line the hole with 3/16 in. brass tubing and cut through both wood and tubing for a lined spacer. When the drive shaft is finished, place it in the channel with 1 in. pieces of 3/16 in. tubing at both ends in the front part; you already have pieces in the back section. Glue/brad the covers in place.

4. Cut out the legs. Beginning with the rooster, cut out the legs and drill a 1/8 in. hole centered 3/4 in. from the top. Glue/brad the legs in place, making sure the holes line up. Then do the same with the chick's legs. The bottoms of the legs should be along the line 1 in. from the top of the platform.

5. Cut out the rooster and chick, then drill 3/16 in. holes for the axles where indicated. Line them with tubing. With a file, thin down the front of the rooster to make it lighter. Turn 3/8 in. screw eyes into the tails of the chickens where they will be above the cams.

6. Make the axles. Mount the rooster first. Put a temporary connecting wire in place and test the rooster's movement. Cut out the whirligig tail piece, checking to make sure the rooster's beak falls at the proper place in the feed pile. Then glue/brad the tail in place. Attach the permanent connecting rod.

7. Follow the same procedure with the chick. When the chick is mounted, glue/brad the small grain pile in position. **Remember that the drive shaft is underneath.** Attach the chick's connecting rod.

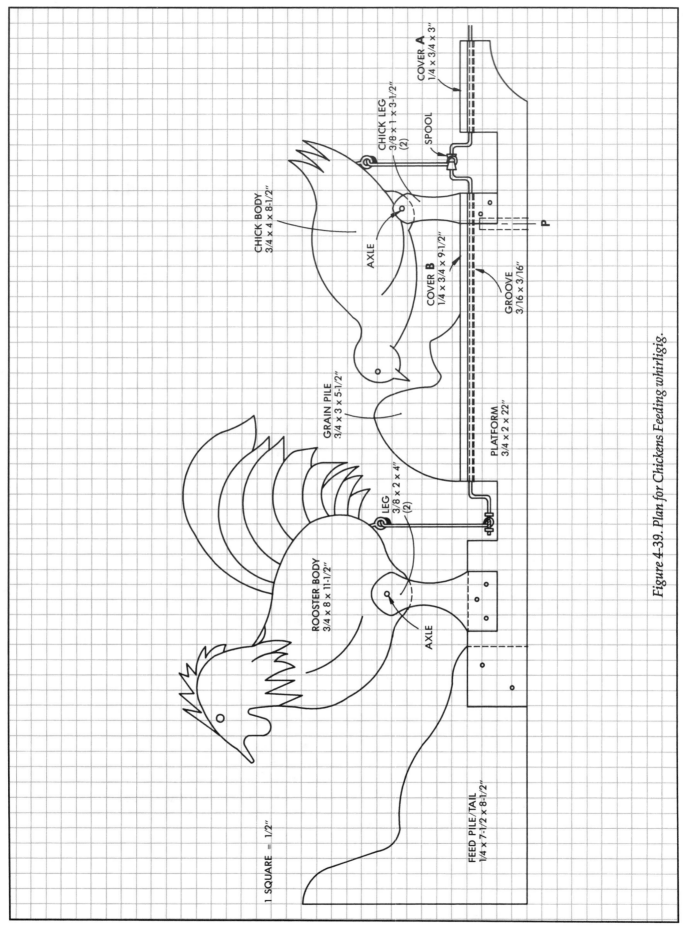

1 SQUARE = 1/2"

COVER A
1/4 x 3/4 x 3"

CHICK LEG
3/8 x 1 x 3-1/2"
(2)

SPOOL

CHICK BODY
3/4 x 4 x 8-1/2"

AXLE

COVER B
1/4 x 3/4 x 9-1/2"

GROOVE
3/16 x 3/16"

P

GRAIN PILE
3/4 x 3 x 5-1/2"

PLATFORM
3/4 x 2 x 22"

LEG
3/8 x 2 x 4"
(2)

ROOSTER BODY
3/4 x 8 x 11-1/2"

AXLE

FEED PILE/TAIL
1/4 x 7-1/2 x 8-1/2"

Figure 4-39. Plan for Chickens Feeding whirligig.

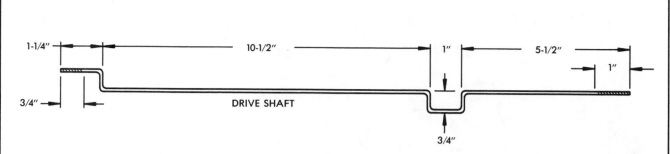

Figure 4-40. Special drive shaft.

8. Construct and install the propeller. The 16 in. cross-lap propeller is best suited to the action of this whirligig. Test the whirligig action.

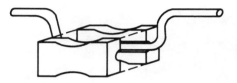

Figure 4-41. Connecting rod spool.

9. Paint the platform green and the grain piles yellow or brownish. Make the rooster many colors, with red predominating, and the smaller chick less striking than the rooster. Paint the chicken legs orange.

Figure 4-42. Saluting the Flag whirligig.

Saluting the Flag

Saluting the Flag (Fig. 4-42) is one of a series of whirligigs characterized by single-arm movements. Although such whirligigs are simple in action, they are fascinating. Their attraction lies in the subject matter and the design (Fig. 4-43).

MATERIALS

Platform: 3/4" x 2-1/4" x 23"
Drive Shaft: 1/8" rod, 7-1/2" long, with 1/2" cam

Support Brackets: (2) 1-1/2" corner irons
Soldier: 3/4" x 2-5/8" x 11"
  Left Arm: 1/4" x 1"x 5"
  Right Arm: 1/4" x 4"x 4-1/2"
Flag Pole: 3/8" x 3/8" x 12-1/2"
Flag: 1/4" x 5"x 6"
Socket Liner: 3/8" tension pin, 2" long
Axle: 1-1/4" No. 6 roundhead brass screw, washers
Connecting Rod: 1/16" rod
Screw Eye: 1/4"

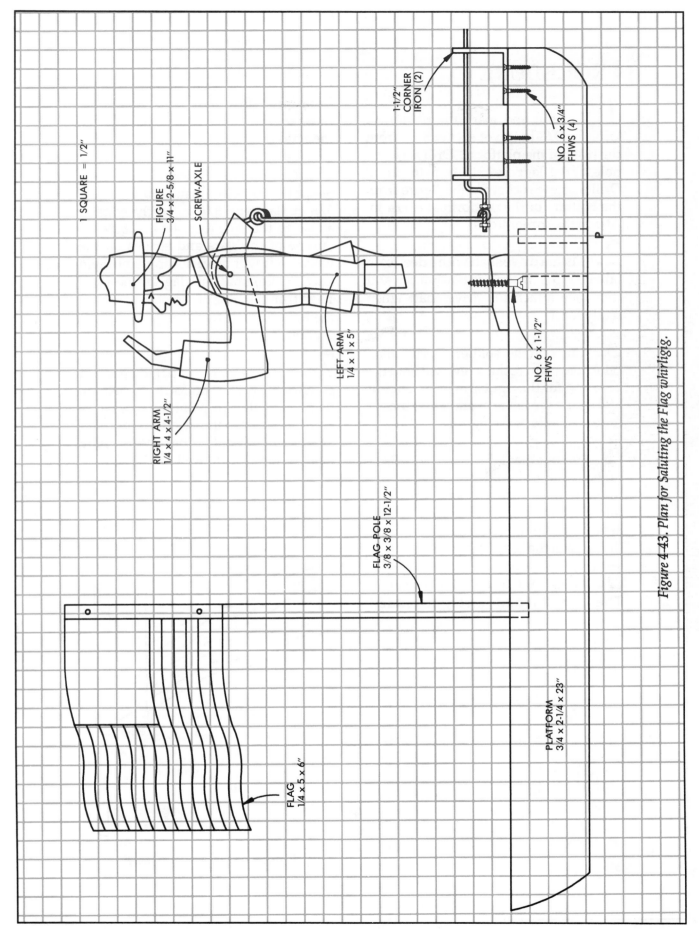

1 SQUARE = 1/2"

FIGURE
3/4 × 2-5/8 × 11"

SCREW-AXLE

1-1/2"
CORNER
IRON (2)

NO. 6 × 3/4"
FHWS (4)

RIGHT ARM
1/4 × 4 × 4-1/2"

LEFT ARM
1/4 × 1 × 5"

NO. 6 × 1-1/2"
FHWS

P

FLAG POLE
3/8 × 3/8 × 12-1/2"

PLATFORM
3/4 × 2-1/4 × 23"

FLAG
1/4 × 5 × 6"

Figure 4-43. Plan for Saluting the Flag whirligig.

PROCEDURE

1. Cut out and mark the platform . Drill the 3/8 in. pivot socket 5 in. from the front of the platform. Drill a 3/8 in. hole for the flagpole 15 in. from the front. Drill a screw socket for the figure from the bottom of the platform at 6-1/4 in. Attach the corner irons.

2. Make a drive shaft with a deep cam (about 1 in.). Insert the tension pin and cap, then attach the drive shaft when ready for it.

3. Cut out the soldier. Drill small pilot holes where the screw will hold the base and for the right arm hub. Cut out and shape the left arm and glue/brad it to the left side of the figure.

4. Cut out the right arm. Drill a 3/16 in. hole in the shoulder and line it with brass tubing. Turn a 1/4 in. screw eye into the rear of the arm piece. Put the arm in position with the screw/axle, then attach the connecting rod.

5. Make and install the propeller. The four-bladed straight-bladed propeller worked well in tests, but in some areas the two-bladed Maltese Cross propellers may be adequate because the arm movement is easy. Check the action.

6. Cut out the flag and flag pole. Shape the flag piece to make a 4-1/4 x 5-5/8 in. flag with 3/8 in. on the edge to attach to the pole (Fig. 4-44). Draw an outline of the stars and stripes on the wood so it will be easier to paint them later. Glue/brad the flag on the pole. Then trim the base of the pole to fit into the hole. Do not glue it in place until it is painted.

7. Paint the platform parade ground green or brown, the uniform tan, and the flagpole white. To paint the red, white and blue, first paint it all white, then overpaint with red stripes and the blue field. White "x"s do well for the stars.

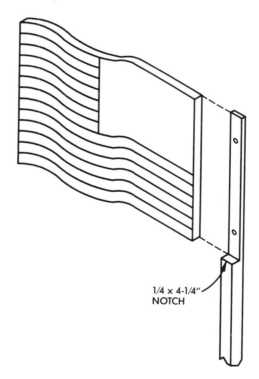

1/4 x 4-1/4"
NOTCH

Figure 4-44. Flag and pole detail.

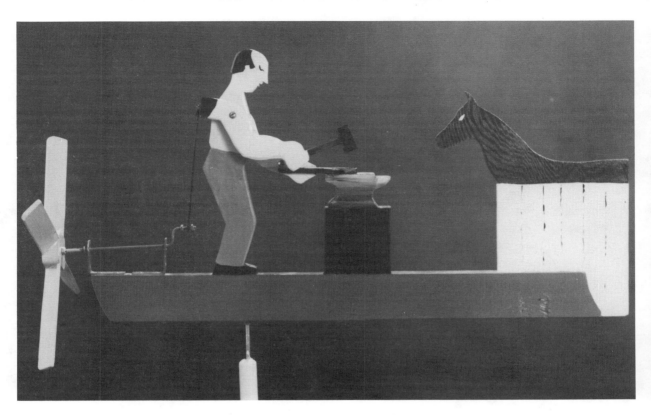

Figure 4-45. Blacksmith whirligig.

Blacksmith

The familiar line, "Under the spreading chestnut tree the village smithy stands" describes an American way of life in the 18th and 19th centuries. It is not entirely a vanished way of life because there are actually more horses now than then, and the modern blacksmith is still hard at work. He does not work under a tree but has a mobile unit and travels to farms and stables, his forge and tools with him. The Blacksmith whirligig (Fig. 4-45) shows him at work.

MATERIALS

Platform: 3/4"x 2-1/4" x 23-1/2"

Drive Shaft: 1/8" rod, 7-1/2" long, with 1/2" cam
Support Brackets: (2) 1-1/2" corner irons
Blacksmith: 3/4" x 2-3/4" x 10-1/4"
  Left Arm: 3/8" x 1-1/2" x 5"
  Pliers: 3/16" x 3/4" x 3-1/2"
  Right Arm: 3/8" x 2" x 5-1/2"
  Hammer: 1/4" x 1" x 3-1/2"
Anvil: 3/4" x 1-1/2" x 3"
Base: 3/4" x 3" x 3"
Tail: 1/4" x 9" x 10-1/4" plywood
Socket Liner: 3/8" tension pin, 2" long; cap
Axle: 1-1/4" No. 6 roundhead brass screw, washers

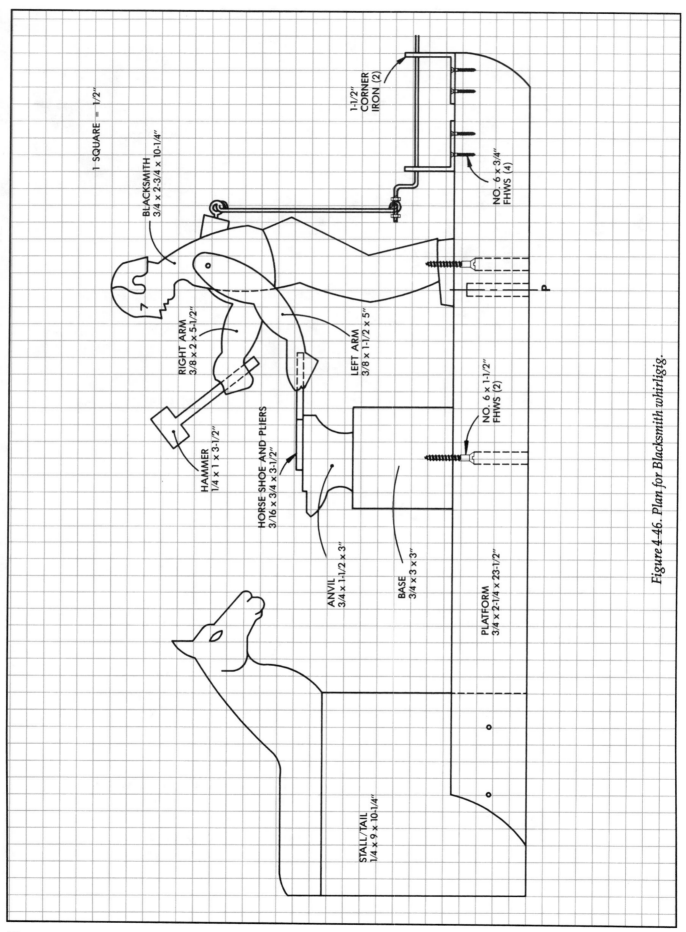

1 SQUARE = 1/2"

BLACKSMITH
3/4 x 2-3/4 x 10-1/4"

1-1/2"
CORNER
IRON (2)

NO. 6 x 3/4"
FHWS (4)

RIGHT ARM
3/8 x 2 x 5-1/2"

LEFT ARM
3/8 x 1-1/2 x 5"

P

HAMMER
1/4 x 1 x 3-1/2"

HORSE SHOE AND PLIERS
3/16 x 3/4 x 3-1/2"

NO. 6 x 1-1/2"
FHWS (2)

ANVIL
3/4 x 1-1/2 x 3"

BASE
3/4 x 3 x 3"

PLATFORM
3/4 x 2-1/4 x 23-1/2"

STALL/TAIL
1/4 x 9 x 10-1/4"

Figure 4-46. Plan for Blacksmith whirligig.

Connecting Rod: 1/16" or 3/32"
rod
Screw Eye: 1/4" or 3/8"

PROCEDURE

1. Cut out the platform and mark the location of the items (Fig. 4-46). Cut a 1/4 in. slot in 4-1/2 in. from the back of the platform for the tail. Drill a 3/8 in. hole for the pivot socket 7 in. from the front of the platform. Drill screw holes for the blacksmith at 6-1/4 in., and for the anvil/stand at 12 in from the front of the platform. Attach the corner irons.

2. Make a standard drive shaft. Insert the tension pin and cap, then attach the drive shaft when ready for it.

3. Cut out the tail and glue/brad it in place. Cut out the blacksmith and glue/screw him in position with the back of his shoe 5-1/2 in. from the front of the platform. Cut out the anvil and base, then glue/screw them in place with the front of the base 10-1/2 in. from the front of the platform and the back at 13-1/2 in.

4. Now make the arms, the hammer and the pliers/horseshoe (Fig. 4-47). Test the location of the left arm and the pliers/horseshoe before attaching the arm to the figure. Cut a slot in the hand for the pliers and glue/brad the pliers to the hand. Then attach the shoulder to the body with glue/brads so that the horseshoe lies flat on the anvil. A brad can hold the pliers/horseshoe to the anvil.

5. Drill a 3/16 in. hole through the shoulder of the right arm and turn the small screw eye to the back end (Fig. 4-48). Cut a slot out of the hand for the hammer handle but do not attach it yet. First put the arm on the body with the screw/axle and see that the head of the hammer falls on the anvil at the horseshoe. Then glue/brad the hammer handle to the right arm. Adjust the connecting rod so the hammer swings over the anvil but does not strike it.

6. Make and attach the propeller. The four-bladed straight-bladed propeller is suitable for this whirligig although in windy areas the smaller two-bladed Maltese Cross propeller will do nicely. Check the movement.

7. Paint the anvil, pliers, and hammer iron gray, the stand brown, and the horse any color you wish. Paint the stalls brown and the platform green or earth color. Paint the blacksmith flesh-colored to the waist in blue jeans.

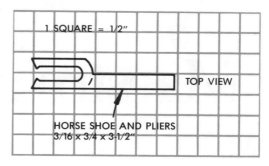

Figure 4-47. Horse shoe and plier detail.

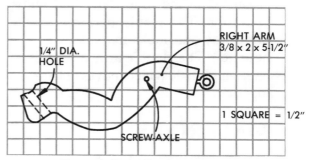

Figure 4-48. Right arm detail.

Figure 4-49. Maestro at the Piano whirligig.

Maestro at the Piano

More complex musicians than the Maestro at the Piano (Fig. 4-49) have been on whirligigs, but they were usually carved in the round and had wide platforms. This pianist performs in the same way and looks marvelous in silhouette. The double-arm mechanism has a single axle which moves both arms together.

MATERIALS

Platform: 3/4" x 2-1/4" x 22"

Drive Shaft: 1/8" rod, 7-1/2" long, with 1/2" cam

Support Brackets: (2) 1-1/2" corner irons

Pianist: 3/4" x 4-1/2" x 6-1/2"
    Right Arm: 3/8" x 1-1/2" x 4"
    Left Arm: 3/8" x 2" x 5"

Piano Legs (2): 3/4" x 1" x 2"

Piano Top: 3/4" x 1-1/2" x 10"

Piano Lid: 1/4" x 5-1/2" x 8-5/8" plywood

Socket Liner: 3/8" tension pin, 2" long

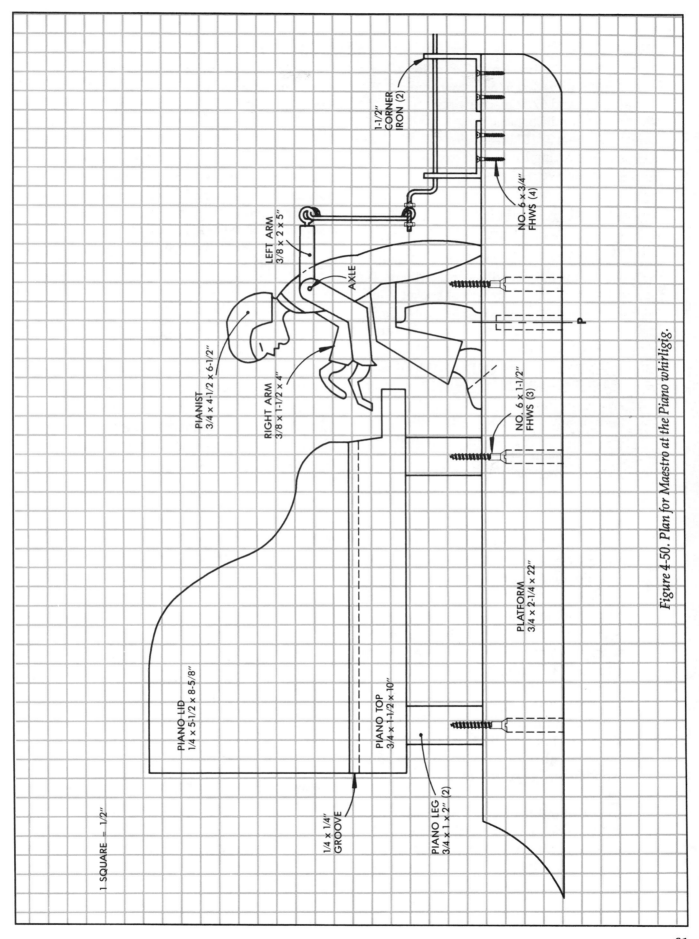

1 SQUARE = 1/2"

PIANO LID
1/4 x 5-1/2 x 8-5/8"

PIANIST
3/4 x 4-1/2 x 6-1/2"

LEFT ARM
3/8 x 2 x 5"

RIGHT ARM
3/8 x 1-1/2 x 4"

AXLE

1-1/2"
CORNER
IRON (2)

NO. 6 x 3/4"
FHWS (4)

P

NO. 6 x 1-1/2"
FHWS (3)

PLATFORM
3/4 x 2-1/4 x 22"

PIANO TOP
3/4 x 1-1/2 x 10"

1/4 x 1/4"
GROOVE

PIANO LEG
3/4 x 1 x 2" (2)

Figure 4-50. Plan for Maestro at the Piano whirligig.

91

Axle: 1/8" brass rod, 2-1/4" long,
  threaded 5/8" at each end,
  and 6/32 machine nuts
  and washers
Tubing: 3/16" brass
Connecting Rod: 1/16" rod
Screw Eye: 1/4" or 3/8"

PROCEDURE

1. Cut out the platform and mark where the objects will be located (Fig. 4-50). Drill the 3/8 in. pivot socket 7 in. from the front of the platform. Drill screw holes for the pianist at 6 in., and for the piano legs at 10-1/2 and 17-1/2 in. from the front of the platform. Attach the corner irons.

2. Make a standard drive shaft. Insert the tension pin and cap and attach the drive shaft when ready.

3. Cut out the maestro. Drill a 3/16 in. hole in the shoulders and line it with brass tubing. Glue/screw him to the platform with his tails 5 in. from the front of the platform. A brad goes through his feet.

4. Cut out the parts of the piano. Secure the legs to the platform with screws and glue with the front edges at 10 and 17 in. from the front of the platform. Cut a 1/4 in. channel in the piano top 1/4 in. deep for the piano lid, then glue/brad the top to the legs, with the keyboard 1 in. past the front leg. Attach the lid with glue. If it is loose, add wooden wedges to secure it.

5. Cut out the arms. Drill both arms in the same place in the shoulders with a 7/64 in. bit. A 1/8 in. bit will do but

the 7/64 in. permits the wood to be turned on snugly. Turn a 1/4 in. screw eye into the end of the left arm.

6. Make the axle (Fig. 4-51). It is the threaded rod for double-arm mechanisms. It uses four 6/32 machine nuts on a 1/8 in. rod, 2-1/4 in. long, with ends threaded in about 5/8 in. Turn the nuts firmly onto the axle. Make sure all are tight. Attach the connecting wire and adjust the arms to the proper position.

7. Make and attach the propeller. The smaller two-bladed Maltese Cross propeller will work the mechanism of this whirligig under most conditions. Test the movement.

8. Paint the platform white, the piano black, and the piano stool brown. Give the pianist a black with white shirt, and yellow or white hair.

**DOUBLE ARM
MECHANISM DETAIL**

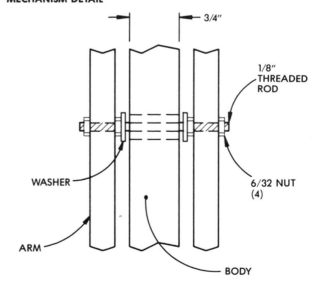

Figure 4-51. Axle detail.

Figure 4-52. Woman at the Computer whirligig.

Woman at the Computer

When I bought my first computer, the word processing instructor asked me if I could make a whirligig showing her at work. I did, using the same mechanism and arm measurements as the Maestro at the Piano for the Woman at the Computer whirligig (Fig. 4-52).

MATERIALS

Platform: 3/4"x 2-1/4" x 21"
Drive Shaft: 1/8" rod, 7-1/2" long,
    with 1/2" cam
Support Brackets: (2) 1-1/2"
    corner irons
Lady: 3/4" x 4-1/2" x 6-1/2"
    Left Arm: 1/4" x 1-1/2" x 5"

Right Arm: 1/4" x 1-1/2" x 3-1/2"
Table Legs: (2) 3/4" x 1" x 1-3/4"
Table Top: 5/8" x 3/4" x 10-3/4"
Computer Base: 1/8" x 3/4" x 3"
Keyboard: 5/8" x 3/4" x 2"
Monitor: 1/4" x 5-3/4" x 7-3/4"
   plywood
Socket Liner: 3/8" tension pin, 2"
   long
Axle: 1/8" brass rod, 2-1/4"
   long-threaded 5/8" at
   both ends, and 6/32
   machine nuts and washers
Tubing: 3/16" brass
Connecting Rod: 1/16" rod or stiff
   wire
Screw Eye: 1/4" or 3/8"

PROCEDURE

1. Cut out the platform and mark where the objects will be located (Fig. 4-53). Drill the 3/8 in. pilot socket hole at 7 in. from the front of the platform. Drill holes to hold the computer operator at 6 in. and the table legs at 10 1/2 and 17-1/2 in. from the front of the platform. Attach the corner irons.

2. Make a standard drive shaft. Insert the tension pin and cap and attach the drive shaft when ready.

3. Cut out the computer operator. Drill a 3/16 in. hole in the shoulder and line it with brass tubing. Then glue/screw the figure in position on the platform and tack a brad through the shoes.

4. Cut out the computer table parts. Attach the legs with glue/screw with the edges 10 and 17 in. from the front of the platform. Cut a 1/4 in. groove along the top of the table top 1/4 in. deep. Glue/nail the top in place, then glue in the monitor. If it is loose, secure it with wooden wedges. Glue/brad the cover in place and secure the keyboard on it.

5. Cut out the arms and drill a 7/64 in. hole through the shoulders. Attach the small screw eye to the end of the left arm.

6. Make the axle with the threaded part slightly longer than usual to accommodate two extra nuts. Attach the arms and nuts to it. Move the arms into an appropriate position, making sure the nuts are tight. Attach the connecting rod and test the arms (see Fig. 4-51 for double-arm mechanism construction).

7. Construct and install the propeller. The two-bladed small Maltese Cross propeller will work well with this whirligig because the action is easy. Test the mechanism.

8. Give the computer operator a bright colored dress with white sleeves. Paint the chair and base of the desk office gray or blue, the table top yellow, the computer keyboard and monitor white, the screen green, and the platform white.

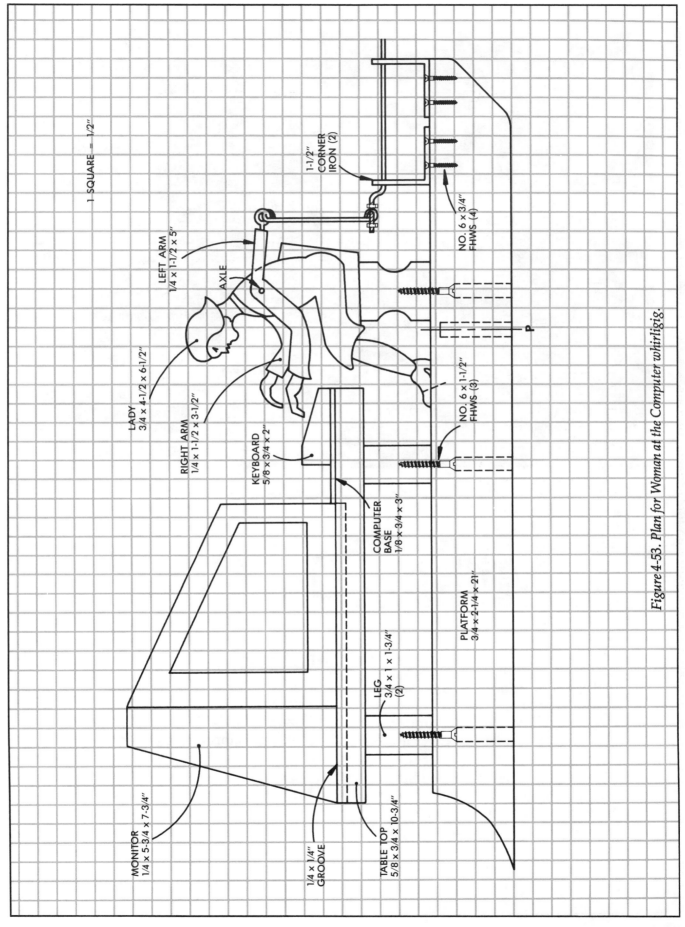

1 SQUARE = 1/2"

LEFT ARM
1/4 x 1-1/2 x 5"

AXLE

LADY
3/4 x 4-1/2 x 6-1/2"

RIGHT ARM
1/4 x 1-1/2 x 3-1/2"

KEYBOARD
5/8 x 3/4 x 2"

COMPUTER BASE
1/8 x 3/4 x 3"

MONITOR
1/4 x 5-3/4 x 7-3/4"

1/4 x 1/4"
GROOVE

TABLE TOP
5/8 x 3/4 x 10-3/4"

LEG
3/4 x 1 x 1-3/4"
(2)

PLATFORM
3/4 x 2-1/4 x 21"

1-1/2"
CORNER IRON (2)

NO. 6 x 3/4"
FHWS (4)

NO. 6 x 1-1/2"
FHWS (3)

P

Figure 4-53. Plan for Woman at the Computer whirligig.

95

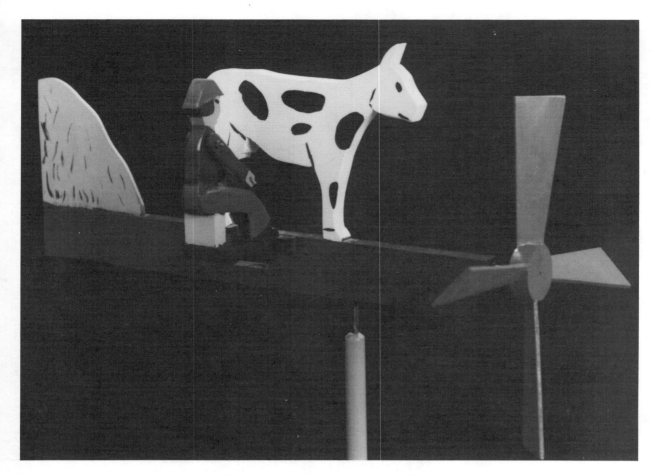

Figure 4-54. Milking the Cow whirligig.

Milking the Cow

The Milking the Cow whirligig (Fig. 4-54) has been around for years, and is one of the more difficult silhouette whirligigs to construct. There is a commercial model that has been around for years and I am tempted to suggest, especially to the beginning craftsperson, that he or she save a headache and buy one. But you will never learn the tricks of the trade that way, so if you want to milk a cow here's how to go about it (Fig. 4-55).

MATERIALS

Platform: 3/4" x 2-1/4" x 19-1/4"
Platform Cover: 1/4" x 3/4" x 10"
Cow: 3/4" x 8"x 11"
Milking Platform: Base 1/2" x 3" x 5"
   Seat: 3/4" x 1-1/4" x 1-1/2"
Farmer-Torso: 3/4" x 2"x 5-1/4"
   Legs (2): 3/4" x 2-1/4" x 4"
   Arms (2): 1/4" x 1"x 4"

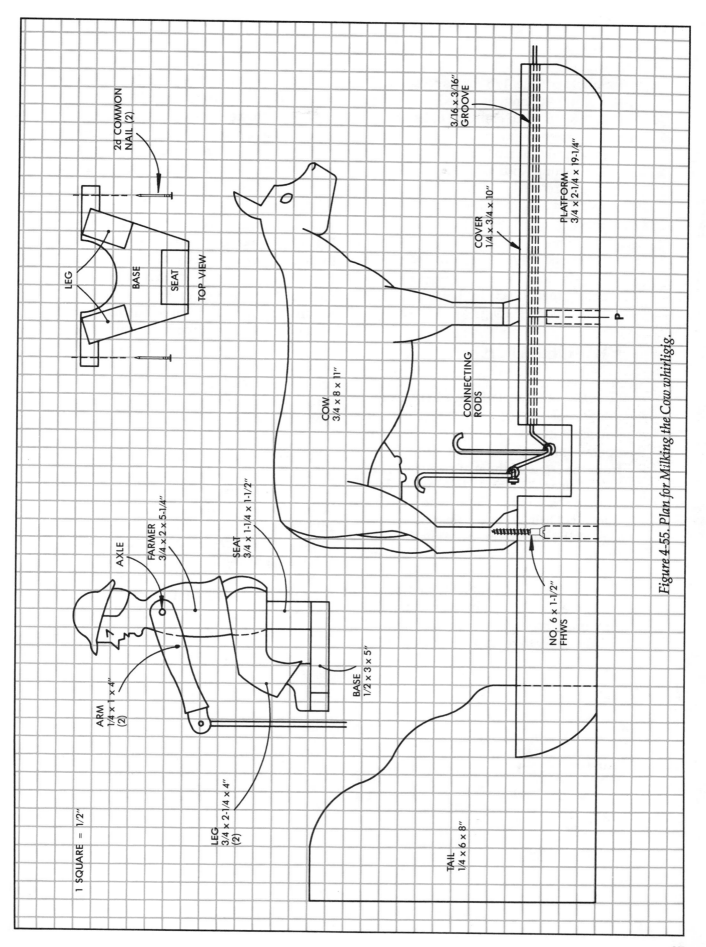

1 SQUARE = 1/2"

2d COMMON
NAIL (2)

LEG

BASE

SEAT

TOP VIEW

COW
3/4 x 8 x 11"

CONNECTING
RODS

3/16 x 3/16"
GROOVE

COVER
1/4 x 3/4 x 10"

PLATFORM
3/4 x 2-1/4 x 19-1/4"

P

NO. 6 x 1-1/2"
FHWS

AXLE

FARMER
3/4 x 2 x 5-1/4"

SEAT
3/4 x 1-1/4 x 1-1/2"

ARM
1/4 x 1 x 4"
(2)

LEG
3/4 x 2-1/4 x 4"
(2)

BASE
1/2 x 3 x 5"

TAIL
1/4 x 6 x 8"

Figure 4-55. Plan for Milking the Cow whirligig.

97

Shoulder Axle: 1/8" brass rod, 1-3/4" long, threaded, 3/16" each end, and 6/32 machine nuts
Tubing: 3/16" brass
Connecting Rod: 3/32" rod or stiff wire
Tail: 1/4" x 6"x 8" plywood
Socket Liner: 3/8" tension pin, 2" long
Drive Shaft: 1/8" steel rod, about 15" long
Shaft Liners (2): 3/16" brass tubing, 1" long

PROCEDURE

1. Cut out the platform and mark the location of all components. Then cut out the 2 in. space where the cam will operate; this reaches from 10 to 12 in. from the front of the platform and is 1-1/2 in. deep. Cut out a 1/4 in. slot 2 in. from the back of the platform for the hay pile tail. Drill a screw hole for the hind legs of the cow 13 in. from the front of the platform. From the front to the 10 in. point, saw off a 1/4 in. strip. Then cut a 3/16 in. channel through the middle for the drive shaft. Test this by placing the 1 in. brass tubing at the ends. Then cut out the cover to replace the cut-off strip.

At this point drill a 3/8 in. hole for the pivot socket 7 in. from the front of the platform. **Make sure you do not drill into the drive shaft channel.** If you do, glue a piece of 3/8 in. dowel in the socket before inserting the tension pin and cap.

2. Make the drive shaft as shown in Fig. 4-56. Make sure cam A is about 1/2 in. above the shaft axis and that B is about 1/2 in. below it. With a metal file, cut out the grooves or small notches around the cam. The slot or notch need not be too deep nor broad. Position the drive shaft, then cut it with a 2 in. protrusion from the platform. Thread this end 1 in. and place it in the channel with the 3/16 in. metal tubing. Glue/brad the cover over it.

3. Construct the milking platform, making sure that it fits across the cut-out on the platform. Attach the milking stool with glue and a nail. Cut out the milker's parts. Drill 1/8 in. holes in the milker's shoulders and arms. Cut away the inside of the legs so they form an angle with the torso, then position the feet at the sides of the cam slot. Glue/brad the shoes on the milking platform, then glue/brad the torso in be-

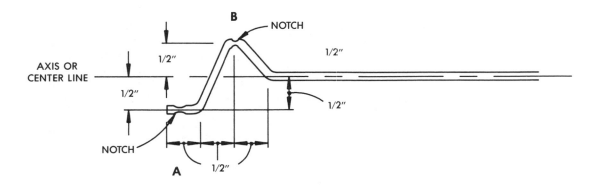

Figure 4-56. Construction of the double-cam mechanism.

tween so it is firmly positioned in the center of the stool. Use plenty of glue on the seat. Drill a hole through the milking platform projection on the left side and secure the milking platform with a 1 in. No. 6 screw and glue. On the right side **(remember that the drive shaft is underneath)** secure it with a 1-1/4 brad driven low.

4. Install the shoulder axle, threaded 3/16 in. at each end, through the shoulders. Position the arms. Cut out the arm connecting rods; make loops at one end and crimp them around the cam slots or cuts. The other ends are bent over and inserted into the hands (Fig. 4-57). Turn the drive shaft to see if the

Figure 4-57. Attaching the farmer's hands.

arms move up and down smoothly and easily. Sometimes they freeze and adjustments must be made. Some bending here and there, or shaving, will usually remedy the problem.

5. Cut out the cow. Farmers will laugh at this ungainly long-legged model, but the milker must fit under it somehow. Position the cow and try the action. You may have to cut away part of the cow or trim the arms if they hit the body. Then glue/screw the hind legs in position and put two brads through the front hoofs, **remembering that the drive shaft is underneath.**

6. The tail is made of 1/4 in. plywood and represents a hay pile. Glue/brad this in place.

7. Build and add the propeller. The four-bladed Maltese Cross propeller with 5 in. blades will work this whirligig. The milking will go on forever.

8. Paint the platform green, the haypile yellow, and the cow brown and white. Give the farmer a red shirt and blue jeans.

5

NON-MECHANICAL SILHOUETTE WHIRLIGIGS

Weathervane Whirligigs

There is a group of non-mechanical silhouette whirligigs in which the propeller doesn't power a drive shaft or make things move on the whirligig. The only thing that moves is the propeller and the platform. Because of this constant movement to face the wind, the non-mechanical silhouette whirligigs are also called Weathervane whirligigs.

The Dutch Tulips whirligigs in this section has the same basic platform as the mechanical whirligigs with the exception that it does not need a tail or a drive shaft. The design provides the tail or rudder effect. The Water Skier whirligig has a standard platform and adds a tail. The Sailboat has a boat hull platform and its sail acts as a rudder, while the River Boat includes a small hull base and a separate tail assembly.

As with the mechanical whirligigs, make the base or platform first, drilling the holes for the pivot socket (P) and for any bottom screw holes. The Skier requires a tail slot. The superstructure of the River Boat will have to be added to the base before the pivot socket can be drilled. When the base is ready, add the other standing features or rudders. The propellers are usually made last because they are positioned after all the other parts are in place.

Non-mechanical silhouette whirligigs are easy to make as there are no inter-related moving parts as in the mechanical whirligig. So, of course, there will be no mechanical parts to get out of order. The secret for an interesting non-mechanical silhouette whirligig is in the subject used for the design. When the subject is appropriate or unique, the non-mechanical or Weathervane whirligig is as interesting as any other.

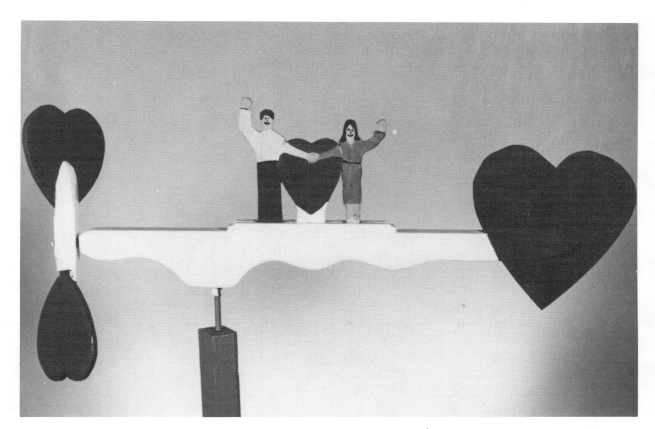

Figure 5-1. Valentine whirligig.

Valentine

A Valentine can be given to a loved one at any time. Many whirligigs are made with hearts, Cupid's arrows, girls chasing boys, and so on. This Valentine whirligig (Fig. 5-1) tells it all.

MATERIALS

Platform: 3/4"x 2-1/4" x 17-1/2"
Tail: 6" x 6" thin metal
Figures: 1/4" x 5" x 5" plywood
Holding Strips: 1/4" x 3/8" x
    6-1/4"
Tension Pin: 3/8", 2" long
Propeller

Arms: 3/4" x 3/4" x 6"
Blades: 1/4" x 3-1/2" x 4"
Screw: 1-1/2" No. 6 roundhead
    brass screw
Tubing: 3/16" brass

PROCEDURES

1. Cut out the platform and mark the locations of the pivot socket 5 in. from the front. The holding strips start 5-1/2 in. from the front, and the tail slot 3 in. from the rear (Fig. 5-2). Drill a pilot hole for the propeller screw. Cut out the tail

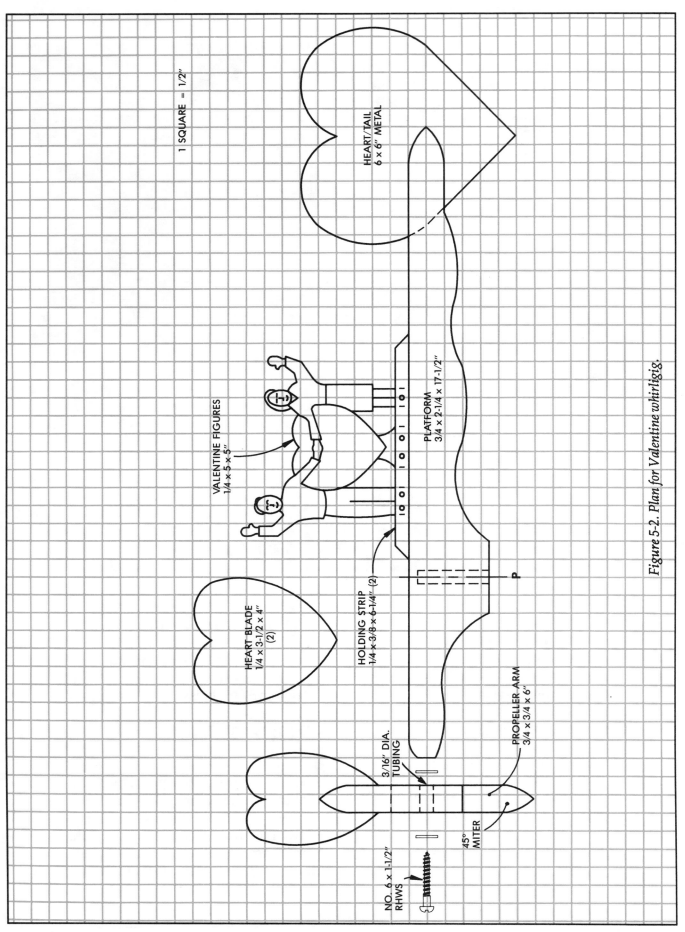

1 SQUARE = 1/2"

HEART/TAIL
6 x 6" METAL

VALENTINE FIGURES
1/4 x 5 x 5"

PLATFORM
3/4 x 2-1/4 x 17-1/2"

HEART BLADE
1/4 x 3-1/2 x 4"
(2)

HOLDING STRIP
1/4 x 3/8 x 6-1/4" (2)

P

PROPELLER ARM
3/4 x 3/4 x 6"

3/16" DIA.
TUBING

45°
MITER

NO. 6 x 1-1/2"
RHWS

Figure 5-2. Plan for Valentine whirligig.

slot with a coping saw. Drill a 3/8 in. hole for the pivot socket and line it with metal tubing or a tension pin and a metal cap at the base.

2. Cut out the figures and draw the details very carefully for guidance when painting. Glue/brad the figures to the platform centered between the holding strips.

3. Make the heart-shaped tail, insert it in the tail slot and secure it with brads.

4. Make the 2-bladed propeller as shown. In the center of the hub, drill a 3/16 in. hole and line it with tubing. Remove 2 in. angled sections from the ends of the arms to hold the heart-shaped blades. You can make a 4-bladed propeller if you wish by using a cross-lap design (see Propeller section in Chapter 2).

5. Try painting the platform white and the hearts red. I painted the woman with an orange dress and the man with blue pants and a yellow shirt.

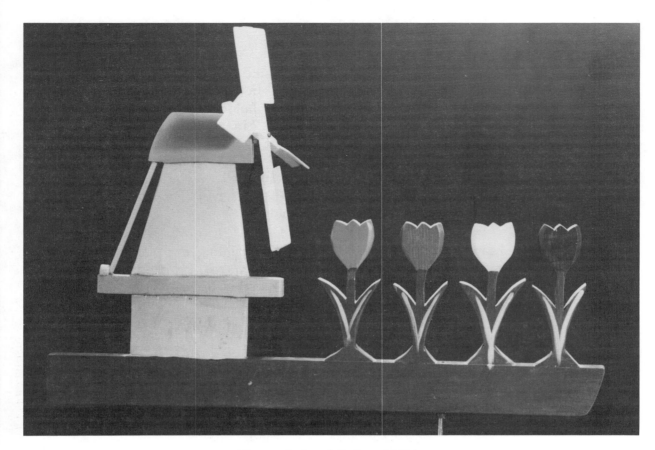

Figure 5-3. Dutch Tulips whirligig.

Dutch Tulips

Dutch windmills by themselves make wonderful whirligigs, but they usually are dimensional copies of the real thing rather than silhouette types. When I thought of making one, I wondered what could use up the space in front of it. Dutch Tulips (Fig. 5-3), of course! So here is a field of tulips backed up by a flat windmill. A friend reportd seeing a marvelous windmill whirligig on which Don Quixote was riding as fast as he could, lance in hand! You can use the windmill theme in many ways.

MATERIALS

Platform: 3/4" x 2-1/4" x 24"
Windmill: 3/4" x 8"x 10-1/2"
Propeller
    Arms/stocks (2): 3/8" x 3/8" x 10"
    Blades/Sails (4): 1/8" x 1-1/2" x 3-1/2"
Tailpiece: 1/4" dowel, 6" long
Tulips (4): 3/4" x 3" x 6"
Socket Liner: 3/8" tension pin, 2" long
Screws (6): No. 6 flathead, 1-1/2"
Screw: No. 6 roundhead brass, 1-1/2" and washers

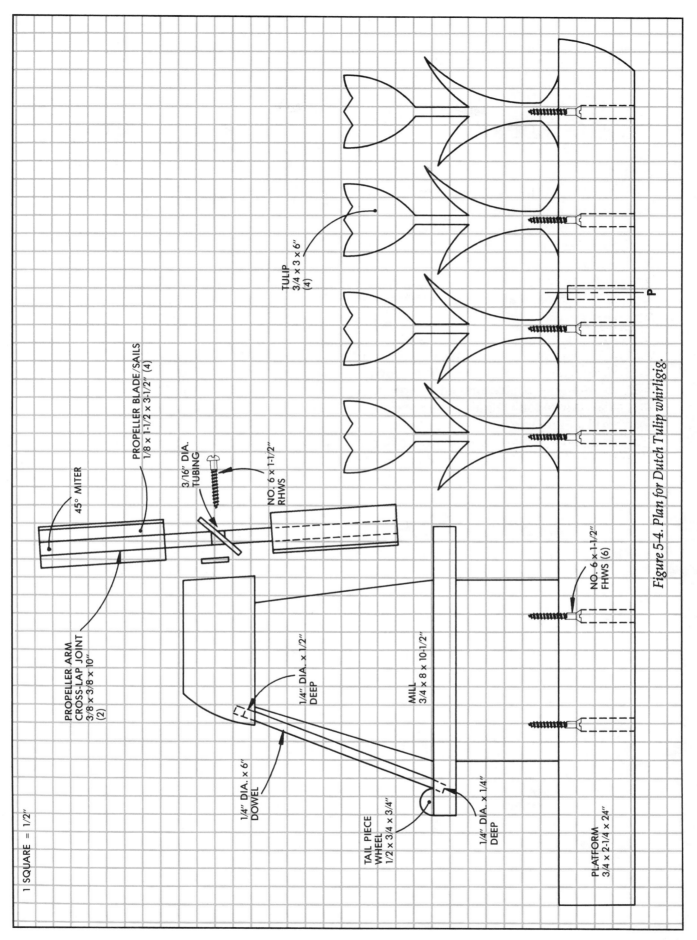

1 SQUARE = 1/2"

PROPELLER ARM
CROSS-LAP JOINT
3/8 x 3/8 x 10"
(2)

45° MITER

PROPELLER BLADE/SAILS
1/8 x 1-1/2 x 3-1/2" (4)

3/16" DIA.
TUBING

NO. 6 x 1-1/2"
RHWS

1/4" DIA. x 6"
DOWEL

1/4" DIA. x 1/2"
DEEP

TAIL PIECE
WHEEL
1/2 x 3/4 x 3/4"

1/4" DIA. x 1/4"
DEEP

MILL
3/4 x 8 x 10-1/2"

TULIP
3/4 x 3 x 6"
(4)

P

NO. 6 x 1-1/2"
FHWS (6)

PLATFORM
3/4 x 2-1/4 x 24"

Figure 5-4. Plan for Dutch Tulip whirligig.

107

Hub liner: 3/16" brass tubing,
1/2" long

PROCEDURE

1. Cut out the platform and mark the positions and center points of the windmill and tulips (Fig. 5-4). Drill screw holes for the 4 tulips at 2, 5, 8, and 11 in. from the front, and two for the windmill at 16 and 19 in. from the front of the platform. Drill a 3/8 in. hole for the pivot socket at 7 in. and insert the tension pin and cap.

2. Cut out the windmill. With a wood chisel, thin the windmill down, maintaining a streamlined shape that will reduce the weight of the windmill. Drill a pilot hole for the propeller screw in the cap at a slight downward slant. Drill holes for the tail and glue it in place. Use wood scrap to make a small half-circle to represent the tailpiece wheel, then glue it by the tailpiece.

3. To construct the windmill propeller, cut out the arms/stocks and blades/sails (Fig. 5-4). Make a cross joint in the middle of the propeller arms. Drill a 3/16 in. hole in the center of the joint. Mark the ends where the sails will be attached and cut off 1/2 of those sections at a 45-degree angle. Glue/brad the sails to the arms and glue the arms together. Insert 3/16 in. brass tubing in the center hub. Mount the propeller with a No. 6 x 1-1/4 in. round head wood screw and washers.

4. Paint the platform green, the tulip leaves green, and the blossoms yellow, red, blue, purple or any other color you like. Make the windmill yellow with the top, balcony, and tailpiece a contrasting or darker color.

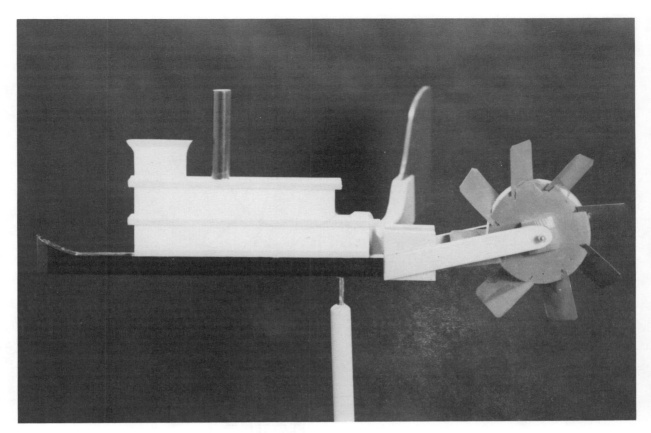

Figure 5-5. River Boat whirligig.

River Boat

The River Boat whirligig (Fig. 5-5) started out to be a show boat. However, they're so ornate with lots of gingerbread, and I knew it would take a long time to do justice to one. Instead I made a basic paddle-wheeler river boat that needs very little decoration (Fig. 5-6).

MATERIALS

Hull: 3/4" x 3/4" x 16"
Bow Piece: 3/4" x 3/4" x 1-3/4"
Superstructure: 3/4" x 4-1/2" x 9-1/2"
Deck Trim: 1/4" x 1/4" cut to fit
Smoke Stack: 3/4" diameter, 4" long
Stern (2): 1/2" x 2" x 2"
Paddle Wheel: 3/4" thick, 4" diameter
Supports (2): 3/8" x 1" x 7"
Wheel Hubs: 1/2" x 1-1/2" x 1-1/2"
Blades (8): 1-1/4" x 2" thin metal
Wheel Axle: 1/8" brass rod, 3-1/8" long, threaded 1/4" at both ends
Tubing: 3/16" brass

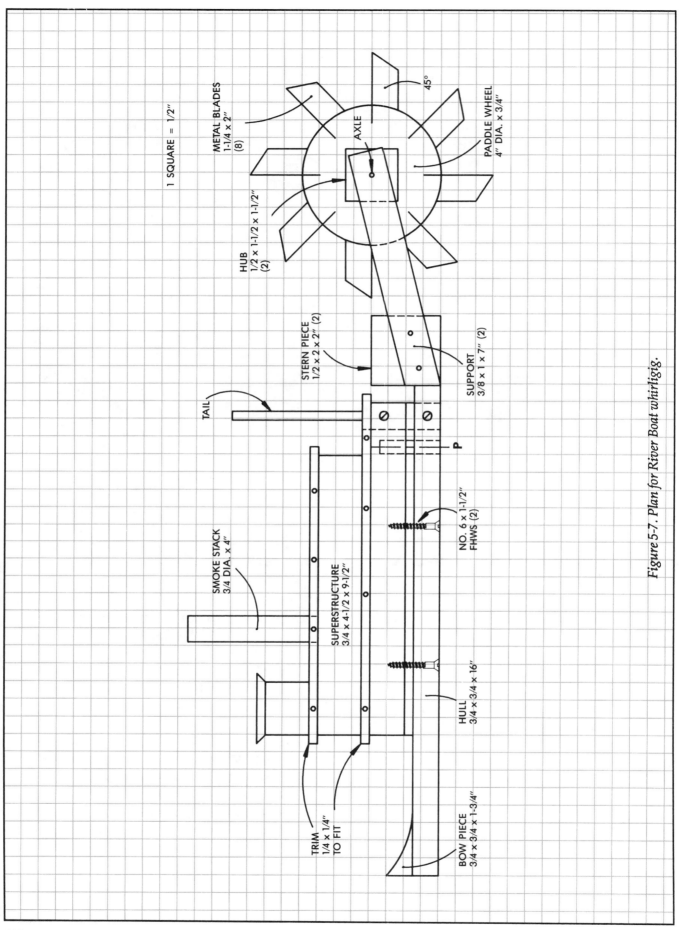

1 SQUARE = 1/2"

METAL BLADES
1-1/4 x 2"
(8)

45°

AXLE

PADDLE WHEEL
4" DIA. x 3/4"

HUB
1/2 x 1-1/2 x 1-1/2"
(2)

STERN PIECE
1/2 x 2 x 2" (2)

TAIL

SUPPORT
3/8 x 1 x 7" (2)

P

SMOKE STACK
3/4 DIA. x 4"

SUPERSTRUCTURE
3/4 x 4-1/2 x 9-1/2"

NO. 6 x 1-1/2"
FHWS (2)

TRIM
1/4 x 1/4"
TO FIT

HULL
3/4 x 3/4 x 16"

BOW PIECE
3/4 x 3/4 x 1-3/4"

Figure 5-7. Plan for River Boat whirligig.

110

Tail, extension: 3/4" x 2-1/4" x 11"
Tail piece: 1/4" x 6" x 8"
Socket Liner: 3/8" tension pin, 2"
    long

PROCEDURE

1. Cut out the hull and the bow piece. Drill the 3/8 in. hole for the pivot socket 12-1/4 in. from the bow. Insert the tension pin and cap. Glue/brad the bow piece to the hull. Cut out the superstructure and glue/screw it to the hull with the front edge 4 in. from the bow. Drill a 3/4 in. hole centered 1-1/2 in. behind the pilot house and glue in the smoke stack. Cut the stern pieces and glue/brad them at the back of the boat.

2. Make the paddle wheel by cutting out a 4 in. circle in 3/4 in. wood. Drill a 3/16 in. hole in the center. Divide the circle into 8 equal parts by measuring off 45-degrees, or by drawing the first line through the center and the second line across it at 90-degrees. Where the lines meet the rim of the wheel, draw 45-degree angles across the edge (Fig. 5-7).

3. Cut down along the edge to a depth of 1/2 in. Next cut the wheel hubs and drill 3/16 in. holes through the centers. Line these up on the paddle wheel and insert 3/16 in. tubing. Spin the wheel on an axle and check to see that the wheel turns straight, then glue the hubs on the wheel with tubing in place. The metal blades can be inserted but not permanently.

4. Cut out the two wheel supports and drill a 1/8 in. hole 1/2 in. from the ends of the supports. Lay the boat on its side. Install one wheel support on the side of the stern piece so the hole is 2 in.

from the base hull line as shown in Fig. 5-6. Place the complete wheel in position with an axle through the hub and hole. Make sure the the wheel will turn without striking the end of the boat. The metal blades should have at least 1/2 in. clearance. Think of the boat in the water. The bottom of the wheel should be at the hull line, with the blades in the water. On my boat, the line down the middle of the support piece to the edge of the stern piece measured 6-1/4 in. to the hole.

5. When you are satisfied the wheel is properly positioned, mark the end of the support piece and trim it. Then glue/brad the first support piece in position. The problem is not measurement, but position. With the axle in place, hold the second support piece so that the axle is level and straight. Mark this position and tack the second support in place. Before securing the second piece permanently, test the turn of the wheel and adjust as needed. When the wheel is properly positioned, mark the end of the second support piece, trim it, and glue/brad it in place. Once the support sides are in place, check the wheel again. If it sticks, file off part of the hubs, and the inside of the supports. Remember that there must also be room for two washers. Now put the wheel aside.

6. The tail is in two parts, an extension and a tail-piece (Fig. 5-8). Cut out the extension and the 1/4 in. slot for the tail, 2 in. from the back. Hold the edge of the extension against the back of the boat, the bottom even with the hull bottom at the back of the lower deck. Mark that position for screws into the extension, then drill two holes for 1-1/4 in. No. 6 screws. They will be approximately 5/8 in. from the back of the boat.

Figure 5-7. Paddle wheel detail.

Then glue/screw the entire tail to the boat (Fig. 5-9).

8. Cut out the 1/4 in. deck trim and glue/brad them in place; the pieces measure 8-1/2 in. on the upper deck and 10 in. on the lower deck. Glue the hull trim pieces along the hull line. Permanently affix the blades in the wheel slots with glue and thin wooden wedges. Before the glue hardens, put the wheel in position once again to make sure the blades do not strike the sides.

9. The boat is now ready for painting. Work boats usually have a black hull, white superstructure, and black smokestacks (I made mine red). The wheel is yellow and the supporting arms metal gray or black. I painted the tail extension white and the river shore line on the tail itself.

7. Cut out the tail piece and glue/brad it into the extension slot.

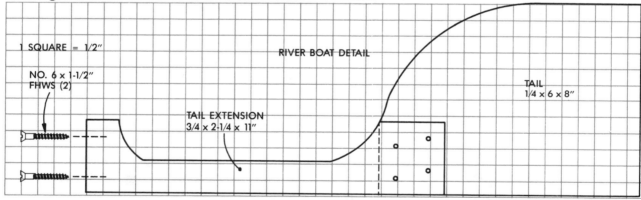

Figure 5-8. Tail piece and extension.

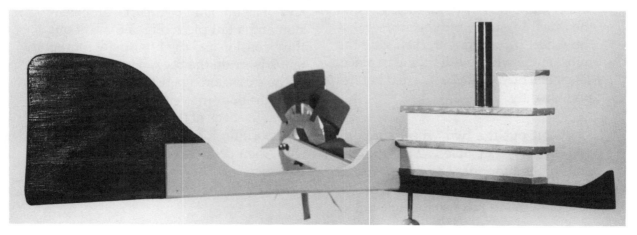

Figure 5-9. Install the tail to the boat.

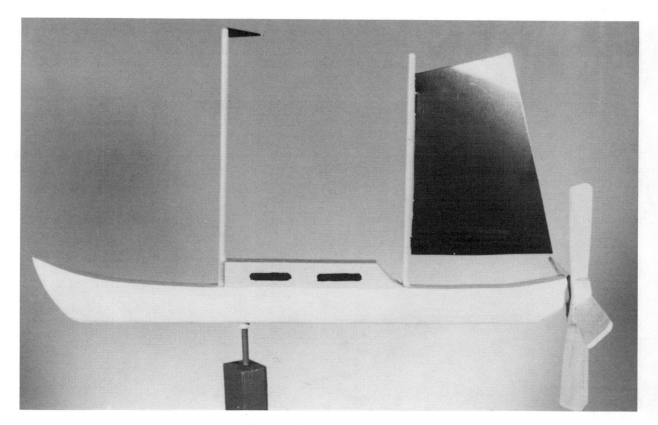

Figure 5-10. Sailboat whirligig.

Sailboat

Ships and boats of all kinds have been subjects for weathervanes and whirligigs for years. Sailboats have been a favorite because a staysail will direct the whirligig into the wind just as it does on an ocean-going vessel.

The first sailboat whirligigs I made were fairly simple. Then I made a large topsail schooner which had five propellers and two drive shafts with lots of action on board. The Sailboat whirligig (Fig. 5-10) project here is a dreamboat schooner rigged with a mizzen sail in place. The propeller at the stern makes it a whirligig.

The Sailboat whirligig is always on the move. You can add sailor cut-outs of 1/4 in. plywood about 4 in. tall to add realism to the whirligig (Fig. 5-11). Include 1/4 in. tabs on the feet for standing figures and on the seats for sitting figures, fitting them into holes drilled into the deck (Fig. 5-12). Attach a small wire from the bow to the stern over the mastheads to add reality to the craft.

MATERIALS

Boat Hull: 3/4" x 2-1/4"x 18"
Masts-Fore: 1/4" dowel, 9-1/2"
 long

Figure 5-11. Sailors add realism to your Sailboat whirligig.

Mizzen: 1/4" dowel, 8-1/2" long
Sail: 5" x 7" thin aluminum
Propeller: 4-bladed Maltese Cross
    3-1/2" blades: 1/4" x
    1-1/4" x 3-1/2"
  Hub: 5/8" x 1-1/2" x 1-1/2"
Tension Pin: 3/8", 2" long, with
  cap
Hub Axle: No. 6 roundheaded
  screw 1-1/2" long, with
  3/16" tubing in hub

PROCEDURE

1. Cut out the boat hull, which includes the cabin, then drill holes for the 1/4 in. diameter masts before and aft the cabin (Fig. 5-13). Drill the pivot socket 7 in. from the bow and line it with tubing or a tension pin, adding a metal cap.

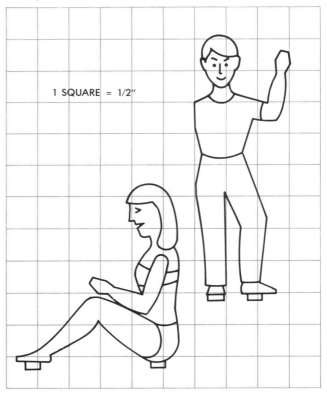

1 SQUARE = 1/2"

Figure 5-12. Sailor detail.

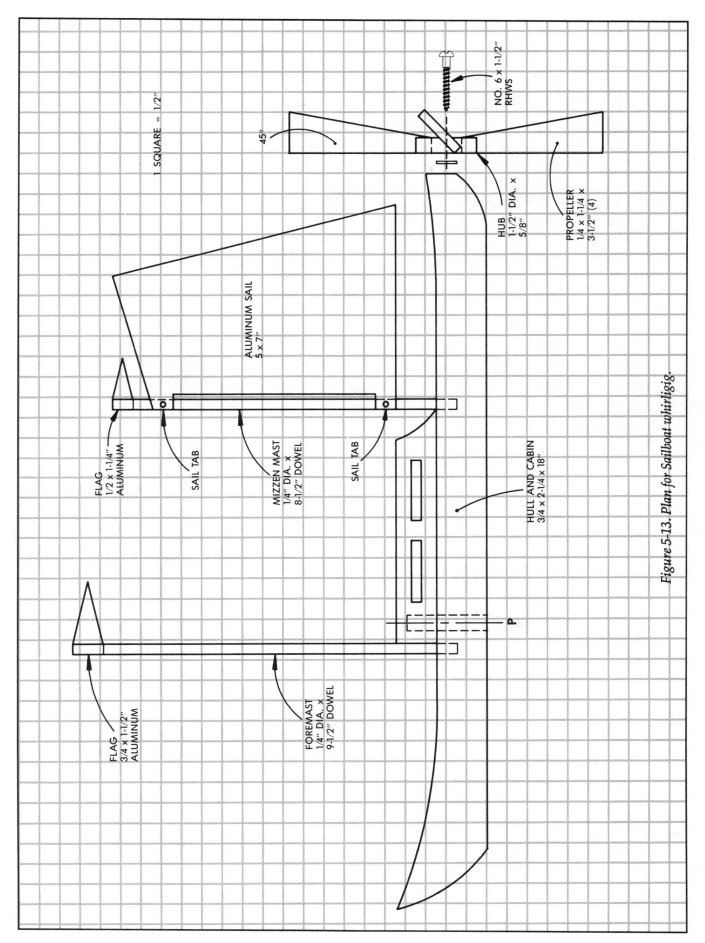

1 SQUARE = 1/2"

NO. 6 x 1-1/2"
RHWS

45°

HUB
1-1/2" DIA. x
5/8"

PROPELLER
1/4 x 1-1/4 x
3-1/2" (4)

ALUMINUM SAIL
5 x 7"

FLAG
1/2 x 1-1/4"
ALUMINUM

SAIL TAB

MIZZEN MAST
1/4" DIA. x
8-1/2" DOWEL

SAIL TAB

HULL AND CABIN
3/4 x 2-1/4 x 18"

P

FLAG
3/4 x 1-1/2"
ALUMINUM

FOREMAST
1/4" DIA. x
9-1/2" DOWEL

Figure 5-13. Plan for Sailboat whirligig.

Drill a pilot hole at the stern for the screw that will hold the propeller in place.

2. Cut out the masts and the sail. The sail has tabs to secure it to the mizzen mast. Using the sail as a measuring device, mark off where the tabs will penetrate the mizzen mast. With a coping saw, or any thin-bladed saw, carefully cut slots in the middle of the mast, top and bottom, where the tabs will fit. Drill small holes through the mast and sail tabs, then secure the sail with small brads cut down to size. Glue the mizzen mast in the rear hole. A small slot can be cut into the top of the fore mast for a flag if desired. Glue the fore mast in place.

3. Construct the 4-bladed Maltese Cross propeller in the same way as shown earlier in Fig. 2-11, but make the hub and blades smaller, as indicated in the materials list. Drill the hub with a 3/16 in. bit and line it with tubing. Attach the propeller to the stern with a 1-1/2 in. No. 6 roundhead brass screw and washers.

4. Paint the boat with classic colors. The hull is white with blue port windows; the cabin and masts are yellow. The sail may be left aluminum colored or may be painted white with red and blue stripes diagonally across it. For fun, the propeller can have varicolored blades.

Figure 5-14. Water Skier whirligig.

Water Skier

The first Water Skier whirligig I designed was pulled by a boat, as ordinarily is the case. To make this one more interesting a pet whale pulls the skier (Fig. 5-14). This design illustrates a kind of weathervane whirligig. It is so balanced that it will always face the wind, and the tail insures that it will. You can make almost any sports subject into a simple silhouette whirligig and after making the skier perhaps you will try to design a whirligig after your own particular interests.

MATERIALS

Platform: 3/4" x 1-1/2" x 20-1/2"
Skier: 3/4" x 5"x 11"
Arms: 3/8" x 7/8" x 4"
Tow Bar: 1/8" rod, 2-1/4 " long
Water Ski: 3/8" x 7/8" x 3-1/2"
Whale-Part A: 3/4" x 4"x 11"
    Part B: 3/4" x 3"x 4"
Nose Propeller: 3/4" x 3/4" x 6"
    (simple two-bladed)
Rudder: 1/4" x 7-1/2" x 7-1/2"
    plywood
Tow Rope: Any stiff wire, 19 to
    20" long

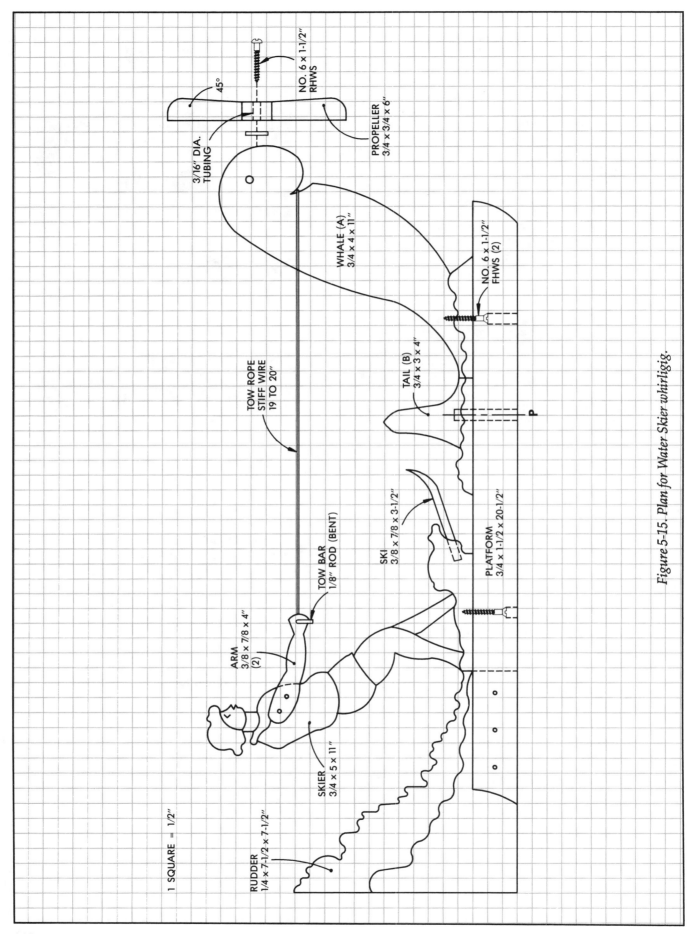

NO. 6 x 1-1/2"
RHWS

PROPELLER
3/4 x 3/4 x 6"

45°

3/16" DIA.
TUBING

WHALE (A)
3/4 x 4 x 11"

NO. 6 x 1-1/2"
FHWS (2)

TOW ROPE
STIFF WIRE
19 TO 20"

TAIL (B)
3/4 x 3 x 4"

P

SKI
3/8 x 7/8 x 3-1/2"

TOW BAR
1/8" ROD (BENT)

PLATFORM
3/4 x 1-1/2 x 20-1/2"

ARM
3/8 x 7/8 x 4"
(2)

SKIER
3/4 x 5 x 11"

1 SQUARE = 1/2"

RUDDER
1/4 x 7-1/2 x 7-1/2"

Figure 5-15. Plan for Water Skier whirligig.

Socket Liner: 3/8"tension pin, 2"
 long
Hub Axle: No. 6 round head
 wood screw 1-1/2" long
 with 3/16" brass tubing

PROCEDURE

1. Cut out the specially-sized platform (Fig. 5-15). Cut a 1/4 in. slot for the
tail 4-1/2 in. from the rear of the platform. Drill a screw hole at 4 in. to hold
whale Part A and another at 14 in. to hold
the skier.

2. Cut out the tail and fit it into the tail
slot. Glue/brad the tail in place. Cut out
the skier. Drill a 1/4 in. hole in the base
for the ski. Then make the arms
separately. Drill a 1/8 in. hole in the
hands for the tow bar. Glue/brad the
arms on the skier. Glue/screw the skier
to the platform. The base should reach
from 12 to 16 in. on the platform and be
tight to the tail. It should appear that the
foamy surf floats up from the skier's
heel. Put the tow bar in place across the
hands and bend the ends.

3. Cut out whale parts A and B.
Glue/screw Part A to the platform, then
nail/glue Part B next to it. Drill a 3/8 in.
hole for the pivot socket 7-1/4 in. from
the front of the platform through the
platform and into whale part B as shown
in Fig. 5-15. Insert the tension pin and
cap.

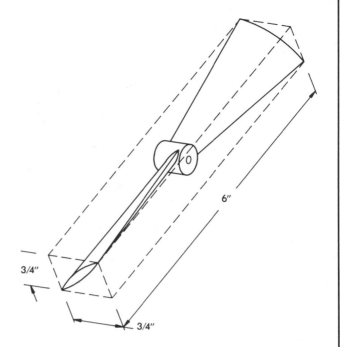

A SIMPLE TWO-BLADED PROPELLER
MAY BE CUT FROM 3/4 x 3/4 x 6"
STOCK

*Figure 5-16. Propeller for Water Skier
whirligig.*

4. Construct a simple 6 in. propeller,
or make one as elaborate as you wish
(Fig. 5-16). The hub of the propeller is
drilled 3/16 in. and has a 3/16 in. tubing
liner. It is attached to the whale with a
1-1/2 in. No. 6 roundhead brass screw
with washers. A stiff wire is stretched
from the tow bar to the whale's mouth.

5. Use your imagination to paint this
fanciful whirligig.

6

DESIGN YOUR OWN SILHOUETTE WHIRLIGIG

Mechanical Whirligigs

Consider inventing your own silhouette whirligig from scratch. Nothing is more pleasing than to see something you design and build flying in the wind. It is relatively easy to make a silhouette whirligig if you have read the introductory section and made at least one of the whirligigs illustrated in this book. Each one gets easier as you go along, and the ideas come faster. Your imagination takes wing and one thing leads to another. You will never run out of original ideas for whirligigs once you have started making your own.

Planning and Sketching

The first step in developing a new whirligig is to plan its design and construction in as much detail as possible. You will start out with an idea about an activity that is interesting, humorous, or exciting. Develop this idea in your mind as fully as possible. Then sketch the figures or objects and the action. Make rough drawings until you have an idea how the parts will all work together. Once you have an idea that you think will work, draw the components full-scale. Don't worry about the accuracy of any figure as long as it is recognizable. One of the problems with my figures is that they are not humorous enough. I think that is because I am so anxious to show people how things work that I tend to keep the characters straight. You can make figures out-of-shape, lopsided, or whatever, and you will make a whirligig that gets attention and makes people laugh. Whirligigs are supposed to be whimsical, amusing and entertaining. The figures you make and the activity they undergo contribute to this goal.

Detailed Drawing

Full-size sketches and drawings will often require paper as long as 24 to 30 inches. If you do not have large drawing paper, simply paste sheets together. I use cheap newsprint paper for my first large sketches and measured drawings. Once I'm ready to make them permanent I transfer them to better paper. A full-scale drawing will enable you to plot the exact positions of the objects or figures on the platform and to plan the action as it will finally take place. This avoids later adjustments.

Start by drawing the temporary platform; temporary because you may wish to make it longer or shorter as you proceed, or you may wish to change the front by adding a platform extension, and so on. Also, you may shift figures and objects around a bit before their final position is determined.

Next come the permanent additions to the platform, such as the support bracket (corner irons or other) and the drive shaft. Then draw in the pivot socket and consider the position and design of the tail.

When this is completed, draw the figures or objects that will go on the platform. When you have the details and the action worked out, carefully measure the final location of the figures and plan where holes will be drilled to hold the figures in place. It's a good rule to make and record measurements from the front of the platform piece. For example, a pivot socket may be at 6 in., a holding screw at 10 in., and a post erected at 15 in.--all from the front end. This makes it easier to locate the pieces when you begin to work on the whirligig.

Pattern-Making

Sometimes it is difficult to estimate how moving figures and related parts (arms, legs, hammers, etc.) will interact. Will they do what you hope they will do? Will the parts reach far enough or too far? If you have a complicated action in mind and are not sure how related parts will work together, try constructing a cardboard cut-out. You can use the pieces later as patterns for cutting out the parts in wood.

Construct Your Model

When you are ready to start on the whirligig itself, make the base or platform first. Adhering strictly to your drawing, use a pencil to mark the locations of the objects and figures that will be attached to the platform. Drill any holes in the bottom for the pivot socket and holding screws, then saw out a tail socket. In some cases you may want to to delay drilling some holes until the final position of the component is firm. This is particularly true when the location of

secondary components depends on the position of a primary component. Following this, add the supports for the drive shaft (platform extension, corner irons, etc). Insert the socket liner and cap. Make the drive shaft and put it in position with the recommended machine nuts in place.

For secondary pieces, attach the moving figure nearest the drive shaft first. Add the moving parts, the axles and the screw eye. Test the action with the connecting rod attached to the drive shaft. When you are sure the movement is correct, add the other figures or objects in their proper position. Your whirligig will be ready as soon as the propeller is attached.

Adjustments

Most whirligigs require minor adjustments once they're assembled. However, when a whirligig stalls, the creator thinks it is the end of the world. Just take the time to think about how it could go wrong, study the action, and make adjustments. Things that have given me trouble have included:

- loop on the connecting rod too tight
- connecting rod too long or too short
- attached parts not loose enough
- screw eye not in the best position
- binding of figures between supports

Things get a little more complicated if figures are out of balance and there is a weight problem. The propeller may not be able to turn the drive shaft. To solve this, figures can be trimmed down or a larger propeller can be used. It is best to take care of the problem of balance and weight distribution in the original design. But even after assembly is not too late.

Non-Mechanical Whirligigs

Much of what has been discussed above applies to the mechanical silhouette whirligigs, but the same process applies to non-mechanical whirligigs as well. These also require planning and design, and the production of a detailed, measured drawing before construction. With the non-mechanical types, drive shafts and their support systems are not necessary, and the primary problem is balancing the whirligig so that it always faces the wind. If the figures or objects themselves do not act as a rudder, then a special tail must be added. This is not a problem. Many unusual weathervane whirligigs are possible including one with numerous propellers spinning away. Such whirligigs always attract attention.

Painting

Be imaginative when painting your whirligig. Use bright paint and make the whirligig outstanding. While many antique traditional whirligigs had somber colors, just as many were brightly colored. Some whirligigs are elaborately painted. Recently in North Carolina, I saw a finely-decorated, multi-colored whirligig of Elvis playing his guitar. You can make your whirligig a work of art as well as a craft project.

Other Whirligigs

While the silhouette whirligig has been the focus of this book, there are many other types of whirligigs. All are fun to make, and only the most complex are difficult to construct. While you will get considerable satisfaction from making a whirligig from plans, you will get even more pleasure from designing and constructing your own. Nothing compares to the feeling of accomplishment when you see your whirligig turning in the wind, and watch others enjoying it too.

Keep 'em flying!

INDEX